SECRET
AND
PERSONAL

F. W. WINTERBOTHAM, C.B.E.

Chief of Air Intelligence of the
Secret Intelligence Service

1930 – 1945

WILLIAM KIMBER
6 QUEEN ANNE'S GATE, LONDON, S.W.1

First published in 1969 by
WILLIAM KIMBER & CO. LIMITED
6 Queen Anne's Gate, London, S.W.1.

© F. W. Winterbotham, 1969
SBN 7183 0321 0

MADE AND PRINTED IN GREAT BRITAIN BY PURNELL & SONS, LTD.
PAULTON (SOMERSET) AND LONDON

Contents

To my children
Pam, Tony, Sue
and Sally

Preface

Towards the end of the mad nineteen twenties, perhaps due to reaction or maybe because the younger 'World War One' generation were growing up a bit faster than their parents and taking more notice of the world around them, there was a feeling of unease and restlessness. We began asking ourselves whether this was in fact the land fit for heroes to live in? Was everything going aright, or were we being lulled by platitudes and pipe-smoke? Was soul-destroying unemployment the reward of years of mud and sacrifice? Which way was a rudderless Europe drifting?

Communism in Russia was settling down after its orgy of genocide and with a crude but partially effective propaganda machine was telling the world what miracles she would achieve with five-year plans and vast armed forces. Some wagged their heads and recalled that France had become fairly normal within fifty years of her revolution; why not Russia? Others wondered what would happen if the Russian millions were really organised; would they dominate Europe? The United States of America, not yet fully conscious of a hostile ideology, was supplying machinery and technical assistance to the U.S.S.R.

We had successfully weathered our own minor revolution, the General Strike. A number of young men had formed themselves into a British Fascist movement; the whole atmosphere was so totally different from anything our fathers had experienced in the well-regulated Victorian day that the elderly politicians did not seem to know which way to turn; they did not turn, they sat very tight and let the mood of the young men and women flow over them.

After my teenage war in the air and eighteen months of a

7

prisoner-of-war camp, which had temporarily knocked the wind out of me, I had taken a law degree at Oxford and then turned to agriculture. By 1928 farming was in the depths of depression. The Government could not have cared less; they were even doing everything to get young men to go to Kenya and Rhodesia. I went to see these places but the story was the same—the world's financial troubles had so depressed raw material prices that there was general gloom in Africa, too. (Luckily I did not stay there to be let down by yet another government in the 1960's.) I returned to England to find that in America the frothy bubble of prosperity was about to burst. A little square man in a black shirt and an absurd tassel on the front of his hat was making a lot of noise in Italy. In London a sort of elderly businessmen's government was still unable to jump the gap between 1914 and 1930. Young Anthony Eden, who had been at Oxford with me in 1919, seemed the only bright star in the political galaxy.

It was time to get a job, preferably a bit closer to the heart of events. It was time, too, to take stock of my qualifications.

I had had a normal upbringing at the beginning of the twentieth century, in a lovely part of the Cotswolds where one learnt to ride and hunt, to shoot and fish, play cricket and golf and generally to behave as if the gay and pleasant life would go on for ever. In 1913, at sixteen, I had been taken away from public school for six months due to growing too fast and sent around the world.

I shall always look back on this experience as one of the most fruitful times of my life. I think at sixteen one is ready to absorb both quickly and accurately so much that slides by when one is older. I still believe that if young students of all nations could be sent all over the world on short exchange courses, prior to their going to university, it would in time put the wrangling of the so called 'United Nations' to shame, give youth both the excitement they need as well as an education comparable to two years at school. The cost? No more than their present education. The value? To my mind, incalculable in its immensity. How much better than pouring foreign aid into unknown bottomless pockets.

As for myself, I am convinced it gave me not only the ability and assurance to talk on equal terms with 'bigwigs' and 'small fry' of every description, but to talk intelligently about far-away places and prospects, a subject which always has a ready audience.

My first trip on an ocean liner; the *Old Laurentic*, now, alas, at the bottom of the Atlantic. The engaging Canadian boy who had just 'done' London, and wanted me to identify for him all the corners of the Tower which, of course, I had never visited but didn't like to say so. His father, the largest jeweller in Montreal who spent patient hours telling me just what to expect in Canada, a calm, delightful person who nearly went mad with excitement when he first saw the trams or 'street cars' in operation in his beloved city; Pemberton, the king of real estate in British Columbia, silver-haired and courteous; other Canadians spoke his name with bated breath; the long journey by Canadian Pacific across Canada; hold-ups where the line had been washed away; my first taste of lumbering when I stopped off at a little station at the foot of the Rocky Mountains to help a friend who had just emigrated to try to clear enough ground on a free gift mountainside to grow enough food for himself, his Swedish helper and his horses. He had built himself a splendid log house, but felling trees and tearing up their roots with the horses, from six a.m. till dusk at twenty degrees below zero was tough.

The charm of Vancouver Island, and ever and always the tout trying to sell you real estate; even the 'Bell Hops' in the hotel had a 'lot' to sell up on the Peace River. The excitement at the surge of expansion was catching, alas, World War I put a stop to it, nor was it able to draw again on that vast reservoir of young men who died in Flanders.

The rhythmic twang of a Hawaiian guitar band floated across the still waters of the docks at Victoria, B.C. as the great new Canadian Pacific ship *The Empress of Asia* slid gently alongside. The haunting music inviting one into this splendid liner. I remember we were a bit late getting under way as we had to take on some one thousand ancient Chinese who were going back to be buried in their homeland. We also took on a vast amount of embalming fluid, so the ship's doctor told me.

Japan in 1913, unbelievably Anglophile, strange and fascinating, not yet emerging into a nation crazed for war by its rising sun. I nearly got arrested for not casting my eyes down when passed on a station platform by the Emperor's uncle. Shanghai: the Union Jack proudly flying over the British Concession. Half an hour I spent watching a bit of a forty-eight-hour run of a Chinese drama.

The Chicago White Sox and the New York Giants, plus their wives doing a world baseball tour, they were going to show the world. We travelled on the same boat to Hong Kong—noisily.

The 7,000-ton Kumano Maru, Japanese line from Hong Kong to Sydney. In those days these ships carried English captains to reassure the dozen or so passengers. Fortunately the Japanese officers were good, the captain was seldom sober. The fabulous days in the South Pacific after the tail of a typhoon had hit us in the China Sea. Calm blue waters, flying fish, coral islands and all. The German traveller who was going to introduce Flit fly spray to Australia: it was a walk-over.

Townsville, Brisbane, Sydney harbour. A trip in a small boat to a deserted beach called Manly; and then what I had come to Australia for, to be a jackaroo on a sheep station of two and a quarter million acres, in the outback, 180 miles over sandy scrub from the trail head; thirty miles from our nearest neighbour; kangaroos, all manner of cockatoos and parakeets; gum trees, and iguanas, mosquitoes and flies. Riding, riding, riding, sheep, sheep, sheep, about one every ten acres; the tough, friendly aboriginals; the English padré, friend of mine host, who started every sentence with 'I don't think I know'—he taught me a lesson. The station manager, Mr. Tapp, a large, fair man who, when we finally took him to Adelaide, thought the sea was a mirage; the Arab and his camel train who came to collect the wool. The stage-coach which delivered mail and stores once a month. What young man would pass up a chance like that unless he preferred psychedelic sex beat?

I saw the fashionable suburb of Auckland in New Zealand which had once been the farm of my grandfather. I saw a large milk-white lake which had disappeared when I was again in the country in the 1940s. I caught 10lb trout. I learned all about the agriculture of the country; the dairy herds and the lamb from the Canterbury Plains. Dunedin, that little bit of pure Scotland; it was Sunday, there was no one even in the streets.

Tasmania, that jewel set in a windy ocean, everywhere I met and talked with as many people as I could, and on the long trip home, on an old P & O Liner run like an army barracks. I wrote up and digested all that I had learned. I also crammed my Greek and my Latin and Paley's *Evidence of Christianity* for my 'little go' exam for Cambridge.

This is not a biography, it is a short story of some of the experiences which helped me do the job I was to get. It had cost my parents under £200, in 1913. I had scarcely had time to take my 'little go' and eat a dinner at Trinity, Cambridge, before the Kaiser launched World War I.

I suppose it was the ambition of a great many young men of my age to fly. Ever since the Wright brothers first took off, I had got as near as I could to an aeroplane. I helped the ill-fated Gustav Hamel when he did a demonstration flight near my house in Gloucestershire. I watched a Frenchman fly upside down at Brooklands and it was only the persuasion of my family and friends which took me into the cavalry instead of the Flying Corps in 1915. Perhaps my love of horses was as strong as my desire to get into the air, anyway at seventeen I found myself a subaltern in the Royal Gloucestershire Hussars Yeomanry, with a couple of chargers I had selected from the depot, a soldier servant and a cavalry troop of my own. Many of my fellow officers were my friends and the men the real yeomen of England, farmers and farmers' sons.

I joined the regiment at camp in Cirencester Park in the spring of 1915. It was fabulous to come straight from school to real live cavalry training. Later in 1916, on the East Coast I was to form and train my own squadron from virtually unbroken Canadian horses and a splendid collection of boys from Bristol who had never ridden anything but bicycles. Gradually they fitted together but just when I had got a really smart squadron the blow fell. Cavalry were no longer needed. I think there was scarcely a dry eye the day they took our horses away. To cap it all we were issued with bicycles—and I got my colonel's permission to join the Royal Flying Corps.

Preface

It was the autumn of 1916 that I went to Oxford to learn the mechanics of flying and had my first flight in a Maurice Farman 'Rumpety' from Port Meadow where later, in 1918, I was to help restart the Oxford Polo Club. I learned to fly on a 'Rumpety', that contraption of struts and spars and vast canvas wings, and a top speed little better than a galloping horse. Soon I graduated to a single-seater Sopwith 'Pup' and, after a total of some fifteen hours in the air, I went to France. To have good hands with a horse was a great help to flying a small fighter aeroplane in 1917. No. 29 squadron which I joined on April 29th, was equipped with French Nieuport Scouts, my C.O., who was all of twenty-one years old, told me to get in and take off, with a warning that it was unlike anything I had ever flown and would swing round in a left-hand circle unless I was careful. I was very careful. In the early summer of 1917, von Richthofen and his boys were throwing their weight about the skies of the Western Front. I survived nearly three months and finally got shot down on Friday, July 13th. My lucky day. I had got away with being, like my aeroplane, slightly 'crumpled' after landing in a shell hole on the German side of the lines.

Well, I had had my flying, and also some of the most exciting and exhilarating days of my life and, as it turned out, the most useful.

In 1929, after my farming effort, I had spent six months trekking through Africa from the Sudan to Cape Town. I had shot big game. Learnt to understand the simple, joyful African and to study the life and prospects of the White Settler. I had a B.A., Oxon, in law and could speak tolerably good French and German.

What sort of a job would all this help me to land? I landed the chance to create and fulfil one of the most fascinating jobs a boy could dream about or a man undertake.

For some years now the press and the broadcasters have been bandying about various symbols of military intelligence. Some books have been more candid in their revelations. The war-time exploits of those gallant men and women of the Resistance have been well and realistically told.

My narrative may at times seem a little bizarre. I have tried

Preface

to throw a few sidelights on some of the people whose ideas, ambitions and actions were to affect the lives of all of us. If I relate conversations I had with people, such conversations will be accurately repeated, but I cannot always vouch for the veracity of the speakers.

Finally, I would like to express my sincere thanks to the Controller of Her Majesty's Stationery Office for permission to quote a letter of 5th July, 1940, written by Major Sir Desmond Morton. It was the latter who first put Barnes Wallis on the Downing Street files. My thanks are also due to Dr. Norbert Wiggershaus of Bonn University for so kindly making known to me items from Rosenberg's diary and reports, and to Musterschmidt Verlag for allowing me to quote from them.

1

The Secret Service

'Vicky—get me the Cabinet Offices on the scrambler, please.'

'That you, Cox? May we scramble? This is Zero C speaking. Just to let you know the first bombs fell on Warsaw a few minutes ago—yes, that's all—don't stay up too late.'

It was already about 2 a.m. on that young September Sunday morning and Cox would be spending most of the rest of the night on the phone. As I replaced the green telephone and lay back on the camp bed in my office, the tension of the past few months seemed to relax a little. The ghastly inevitability of this moment had grown step by step over the past six years and now World War Two had begun.

We had, of course, known the approximate date for some months past so that there was no sense of shock and now that it had finally happened I found my thoughts ranging back over the past decade. Would it be a repetition of World War One? No! the Nazis could never afford to get bogged down in the West. How could we possibly cope, with our virtually unarmed 'armed forces'? Could it have been avoided? Why had our politicians of the 'thirties failed so utterly, both in diplomacy and rearmament, to deal with the gangsters of Berlin? One thing is certain; it had not been for lack of information.

My mind went back to the day when I had first walked down the thickly carpeted passage to the soundproof doors not far from where I now lay resting and my first conversation with my future chief, the Admiral.

As he got up from behind his large mahogany desk to greet me, I saw a rather short, stocky figure, dark of countenance, with a welcoming smile in the manner of a benign uncle. His handshake was gentle, as was his voice, and only the very alert dark eyes gave any hint of his tough personality. I remember the first piece of advice he ever gave me.

'If,' he said, 'you can listen to someone important telling someone else important about some event of importance and, knowing the story to be quite inaccurate, you can keep your mouth shut, you may in due course make a good intelligence officer.' Whereupon he put a bowler hat which was rather too small for him as firmly as possible on his head and went off to see the Prime Minister.

So this was 'C', and I was being accepted as a member of his staff and of the Secret Service. Admiral Sir Hugh Sinclair ('Quex' to the Navy) was not only my chief but my friend and adviser for ten crowded years. His absolute personal loyalty and fairness to his staff was a quality rarely found in these days of government by committee and shared responsibility.

During my long fights with the governments of the day to get the facts and figures of German air rearmament accepted, he never once failed to back me up. On one vital occasion when my job was at stake, his favourite phrase 'there has been a decided absence of clear thinking in this matter (on behalf of the Government)' changed the fates of at least one cabinet minister and saved my own head. He set me a standard I never forgot, of controlled authority.

It was at the beginning of the 1930s. I had had to dig myself out of the snow in order to get away to London from my Cotswold farm. And now I was to work in an office somewhere in Whitehall. I wondered how I should take it but I need not have been worried; I cannot remember a single day during the fifteen years I spent in my job when I didn't look forward to every minute of it. Often I was away travelling, often I was in the office day and night, but from beginning to end it was absolutely enthralling.

During the 1920s the Royal Air Force had been so busy reshaping its large wartime organisation and building a well-trained, well-armed peacetime service that it had had little time to build up an intelligence department, but now, at the beginning of the 'thirties, ambitious men abroad were once again stirring the ugly brew of power and new excuses were being thought up for pushing other people around.

The R.A.F. now had its rightful place alongside the other fighting services, in the plans for the defence of the nation and the still existent Empire. To make plans one must have knowledge of the strength and ambitions of any potential enemies, and much of this sort of information can only be acquired secretly. Obtaining such secret information for the Air Staff was to be my task in my position of Chief of Air Intelligence of the Secret Intelligence Service.

It was not going to be easy. People who had the required technical knowledge and were willing to talk would be hard to find. I should not only have to find them but train them in the sort of intelligence I required. From my knowledge of the agent and from my own knowledge of the subject I should have to judge the accuracy of the information supplied, and I must know and understand all the varied requirements of the Air Staff and the people who would use the information and be able to guide them as to its accuracy and assessment—no small job to start up from virtually zero.

It is a wise tradition that details of the working of the Secret Intelligence Service should not be made public and, as little as twenty-five years ago, it was considered an offence even to mention the name or the symbol M.I.6 to an outsider. Times have changed and some authors who were for a while connected with secret intelligence have given accounts of their experiences, often embellished by name-dropping and inaccurate conjectures.

There are many different sources of intelligence but in the years before the war my activities were primarily concerned with the spy.

In the early 1930s it became evident that Germany was the principal 'target' and that not only was time not on our side but the quantity and quality of available spies was becoming strictly limited in a Nazi Germany of national enthusiasm and frightening security. It was then that I found it necessary and stimulating to operate in Germany myself in order to be able to keep up a 'running commentary' to the Government on the progress of German rearmament in the air and, at the same time, try and persuade them to wake up to the realities of what we were in for.

The first part of this book deals, therefore, with my activities as a somewhat privileged agent in personal contact with the Nazi leaders themselves; it also contains the true account of how I and my French opposite number started the original aerial spy project using high altitude photography which, hitherto, had been impossible due to the cold fogging up the lenses of the cameras.

There have been numerous accounts of the exploits of Sidney Cotton; none so far have given all the relevant facts. This was an operation by and on behalf of the Secret Service. The whole idea was hatched by myself and my French colleague.

I obtained two Lockheed 12a aircraft from America—one paid for by the Secret Service, the other by the French Deuxième Bureau. I hired Cotton to fly our aircraft. He was paid a very generous allowance which covered his luxury flat in London, living expenses, the salaries of his co-pilot and mechanic, and all maintenance, fuel and aerodrome costs. All equipment was bought either by the S.I.S. or obtained from the R.A.F., and I had all necessary alterations to the aircraft done secretly through the Air Ministry. Without our experiments and the discoveries we made, the pale eggshell blue spy-plane flying at 25,000 feet almost unseen and unheard above the countries of our potential enemies could not have achieved its great success.

The hidden cameras in the aircraft's 'belly' which automatically took overlapping photographs through lenses kept clear by the flow of warm air from the heated cabin passing over them; the ability to produce stereoscopic results with three-dimensional measurement of objects on the ground; the hundreds of square miles covered by the high altitude cameras during the war and the large and efficient interpretation unit set up to deal with them must have been responsible for a high portion of the top grade intelligence supplied to the allied leaders and commanders in the field.

Came the war, and now, just when his authority and stature were most needed, my old Chief died; his deputy, my military colleague, took over as the new 'C'.

The aerial spy unit was taken over complete and was made an official unit of the R.A.F. It was given Spitfires and a serving C.O.

It is inevitable that on the outbreak of a shooting war involving a number of countries, the waves of security and spy-hunting force the ordinary peace-time secret agent to go to ground, for a time at least. Communications are disrupted and whole populations are on the move; much will therefore depend on the sort of pipelines of intelligence that it has been possible to lay in peace-time. It was in 1940 that one such pipeline provided us with evidence that there would be possibilities of considerable, if intermittent, success against the German cypher machine 'Enigma'.

Cryptography and the operation of secret agents are often interdependent; results obtained from both are of the highest grade of secrecy, whilst the former also carries the highest grade of accuracy. Cryptography, which covers the whole range of breaking the enemy's codes and cyphers after intercepting his signals either in the ether or on land wire, is a science in its own right and demands an extremely intelligent and often mathematical brain, but it can be and often is partly, or even wholly, assisted by the secret agent who will supply copies of messages before they are encyphered, copies of code books or methods of cypher procedure. These are the prime targets of the secret agents of all countries and it is distressing to note how many men and women in this country have been caught in this form of espionage in recent years.

It is evident, too, from the way that we hear of Russian trawlers stuffed with electronic detection gear following our warships around on manoeuvres, of American ships like the *Pueblo* on the same game getting seized by the Koreans, that the cypher business is 'hot'.

Despite all the publicity about spy ships and cypher stealing agents of foreign powers, it is the earnest endeavour of every country to keep the extent of its own successes in this field a close secret.

We were fortunate that, with commendable foresight, the S.I.S. arranged for experts to go into the heart of Germany immediately after the capitulation to recover any documents they could. In this way we were able to find out how far the German crypto-graphers had succeeded with our own cyphers during World War Two. There were certainly some surprises at their successes, especially regarding the naval codes. It was fortunate that a new broom at the Admiralty tightened up the cypher position before it was too late, and but for Commander—now Admiral—Denning, the U-boats would have had a bumper harvest. The R.A.F. produced a cypher machine which was also used by the Army; this was, oddly enough, very similar to the German Enigma cypher machine which was used throughout the German armed forces, but the R.A.F. model had additional safeguards and, as far as we can tell from captured documents, was never read.

Security, both in the distribution and use of the top-grade intelligence from such sources, is vital. 'C' appointed me to act as his deputy for completely safeguarding any such items of information which might from time to time become available.

In this respect I also became his personal liaison officer with the principal allied commanders in the various theatres of operations, whilst at home I was responsible for selecting any item that might become available of such importance as to merit sending direct to the Prime Minister. He in turn asked that I should give him a short note of explanation in such circumstances.

Thus, as the war went on, there was a change of emphasis in my work which gave me a wider responsibility and a chance to meet and know the men on our side who shaped our destinies; I already knew those on the other.

It is therefore primarily with people that the latter part of this book is concerned, together with some memories of the role played by our most valuable and reliable source of intelligence in a few of the vital turning points of the war.

2

Early Days

The story, however, properly begins in January 1930 when I found myself in my small office near Whitehall, sharing an efficient secretary who also played hockey for England, and wondering how I was going to organise this new and exciting job and, above all, achieve results.

Before I could even start to operate I had got to learn about a great many people, international situations and events. The Russians were much in the limelight, especially a gentleman called Zinoviev who was supposed to have written indiscreet letters about subversion in Britain. It gradually became evident that the Russian military menace, far from being imminent, was a carefully contrived bluff. Despite their much publicised five-year plans the Russian peasant was not yet a technician. Nevertheless their exercises in propaganda seemed to bemuse the British Government; they were a foretaste of things to come.

The boisterous Latins in their black Fascist shirts were becoming easier to understand. The British were unused to being at the receiving end of the new mass propaganda of the Dictators and did not quite know how to take it at first. In due course Mussolini stuck closely to Precept Number One of the Rules of Dictatorship —if you begin to grind to a halt at home you must discover a foreign enemy or, even better, engage in a small foreign conquest. The latter had to be a pretty easy proposition if the Italians were to tackle it by themselves. Ethiopia served their purpose but all too soon became international and in due course spawned the abortive Hoare-Laval Pact which, in turn, eliminated Hoare. With the exception of the U.S.S.R. and Italy the rest of the world seemed to be drifting along fairly quietly. For how long?

Meantime an aeroplane had been seen flying backwards in Holland. The matter was investigated.

The American financial crash put the skids under Wall Street and the repercussions in Europe were far-reaching. Unemployment was becoming a virulent disease; there still seemed to be more emphasis on things than people; our somewhat complacent government had plenty of home worries.

The Germans have been taught to be patient, at least the Western Germans. The Prussians are in a different category. It has always seemed to me that the Prussians are so belligerent because their early history was harshly influenced by the Mongolian Conquest. The Huns left their imprint. Further west the more civilising influence of the Latins brought an earlier culture never enjoyed by the more Northern Barbarians, as the Romans called them.

Too many people make the mistake of thinking that the evolution of men's minds has progressed equally all over the world. The human animal can quickly assimilate a veneer which is all too often taken to indicate a civilised state of mind which as yet does not exist—a common mistake amongst the well-meaning but untravelled do-gooders.

It is perhaps because I was thrown so early in life amongst all sorts and conditions of men in all corners of the globe that I learned to observe people more than things. It is people and their motives which interest me and it is about people rather than political happenings that I write. Events have, anyway, been very fully covered already.

But to return to Germany. By the early 1930s all those German babies born in World War One had begun to grow up enough to start looking for something more than the causeless, ineffective middleness begotten by the Versailles Treaty. British youngsters still had the cause of Empire, the possibility of adventure in the Colonies, of administration in Africa, of ruling the waves, of a land of hope if not glory overseas. Rudyard Kipling and pomp and circumstance were not yet taboo.

For hundreds, nay thousands, of years youth has let off steam by fighting, usually the neighbouring tribe or kingdom or country. Wars have thrown up their heroes and then, for a time, youth licks its wounds until another generation grows restless. Unless some new, exciting and constructive ideas are found to relieve the boredom and restlessness of youth, war will go on.

How well the little Austrian corporal gauged the aspirations of the youth of Germany; a curiously sentimental, sometimes almost a mystical people, they desperately wanted a cause and a hero. It was the boredom and disillusionment of the youth of Germany which created the climate for the Nazis to flourish in.

As well as doing my general political homework, I had started to try to find suitable people in Europe with both aeronautical and technical knowledge who could tell me what was going on. Organisation and training of air forces was also a rather specialised subject.

Bits of information were coming through about the way Germany was getting round the Versailles Treaty by training suitable young men in gliding in Germany and then sending them on a short course in Russia where they quickly learnt to become pilots. This was done by a secret treaty between the German generals and the Russians.

Aviation was in a state of rapid development in the early 'thirties and not only could I find few people able to talk about it but fewer still willing to disclose the advances being made in aircraft and aero-engine design. It began to look as if I should have to send people out from England on the pretext of selling British aviation to countries abroad, or else do a bit of travelling myself. In the event I did both.

William de Ropp lived in Berlin. A one-time Baltic Baron, whose lands had been taken by the Communists, Bill was, in fact, very English in his outlook as well as in appearance, nearly six feet tall and solidly built, with sandy hair and moustache, blue eyed, and carefully if casually dressed. He looked the typical Englishman, but could pass as a German or Russian, so perfect were his languages, and often belied the very keen intelligence which lay behind his rather bland smile.

His English wife, a brunette, slim and with deep brown eyes, was almost aggressively British and amused the Nazis by wearing a large Union Jack brooch on all possible occasions! Jimmy, as she was called, was the envy of the not so slim Berlinese of the 'thirties. They lived in a pleasant flat on the Kurfurstendamm, that strange mixture of Piccadilly and the Champs Elysées.

Bill had served in the Wiltshire Regiment and later in the R.A.F. in World War One. He was a close friend and colleague of mine and a lively companion. In one way he was true to type of many of the more intelligent exiles from Russia; he delighted in exercising his mind with politics and had a superb nose for intrigue.

Bill contributed political articles to *The Times* and kept a very sensitive ear close to the ground. It was not surprising, therefore, that he was one of the first people to hear the 'stomping' of the National Socialists way down in Munich. At first he was only an interested spectator of the new movement; nevertheless, it did not take him long to get an introduction to one of the three top men in the Party, Alfred Rosenberg, in order to find out just what was going on. Both were from the Baltic Provinces. Bill was a good listener and soon realised that the new movement would have to be taken seriously.

Rosenberg, on his side, was the principal architect of the Nazi Ideology or, rather, the co-ordinator of the bits and pieces of borrowed ideas which went to make up this philosophy. He also occupied a sort of public relations position in the Party which made him responsible for gauging public opinion abroad in respect of the new movement and trying to influence the Foreign Press in its favour. Bill was therefore right up his street. The association ripened quickly. Rosenberg was a rather lonely, reserved type and there is little doubt that he developed a genuine liking for Bill. Anyone who happened to read the articles about de Ropp in the *Daily Mail* in October 1957 would know how Bill became a close confidant of Rosenberg and this, in turn, led to Bill's advice being sought by Hitler on the subject of English reactions to the Nazis.

Just how close Bill was to Rosenberg could only be judged accurately by seeing them together over a number of years; some idea of their 'friendship' can be gathered from the fact that Rosenberg begged that both Bill and I should go to the Nuremberg Trials to try to save his neck. They often talked and argued far into the night and there were few of Rosenberg's thoughts and ideas which Bill did not know.

The attention given to the Nazi Party by London was small in the early stages and, despite Bill's warnings, the official minds seemed to shrug the matter off as just another political party of little consequence. But as Bill talked to me of the men involved, their aims and ambitions and their appeal to the restless youth, it became evident that here in Hitler might be the prophet, albeit a pagan one, which a frustrated Germany might follow. In any case it would be a good idea to find out a little more about them. Bill suggested that I should invite Rosenberg over to London. He was more or less unknown over here and it was unlikely that his presence would arouse any comment. Rosenberg would be flattered and Bill's position strengthened. It would also give Rosenberg a chance to see a bit of England and perhaps become aware of our preoccupation with trade rather than ideologies or conquests.

I met them off the Harwich Boat Train at Liverpool Street. My first impressions of Alfred Rosenberg as he appeared in London on that late autumn day in 1931 were of a keen, intelligent and cheerful type, rather heavily built, in his late thirties, like myself, height about five-feet-ten, rather coarse features, anxious to make a good impression and, above all, to talk of his beloved movement.

As I listened to this young revolutionary and realised the scope of the new ideology he was proclaiming I became fascinated and alarmed.

We put Rosenberg up in an hotel noted for its excellence. Bill looked after him. As a correspondent of *The Times*, Bill was able to arrange a lunch with the editor, Dawson. This appealed to Rosenberg, for, when the Nazis took over, he was destined to combine the jobs of Minister for Foreign Relations and the Press. This was before Ribbentrop came on the scene as a full-blown Foreign Secretary.

I think Rosenberg was the only Nazi who fully understood, as a result of his early meeting with Dawson, that British newspapers— even *The Times*—are not in any way controlled, at least in peace-time, by the government. Hitler would never believe this and repeatedly used to blame Rosenberg, or so Rosenberg told me, for critical articles in *The Times*, and I gathered he expected Rosenberg to put it right.

I managed to get hold of Oliver Locker-Lampson who, at that time, was running an organisation called the Blue-shirts. I don't really remember what their aims or politics were, but they wore a coloured shirt and this was enough for Rosenberg. He was delighted. Here was a brother revolutionary; what would they not do together when the time came? Poor Locker-Lampson was a bit overwhelmed, but the luncheon he gave us at the Savoy was so good I got the impression that Rosenberg's volubility was coming a bad second to the lobster. This was something to tell his pals about when he got back to Berlin. He sent a large gold cigarette case to Locker-Lampson as a token of esteem. I had the difficult and delicate task of returning it.

We gave Rosenberg the usual run around London and he saw a bit of the Surrey countryside; he went back enchanted with the English manners and friendliness. Bill was 'in' better than ever.

It is recognised in Intelligence circles that after a while one develops a 'nose', whether it be the ability to spot the real thing from the fake, or a feeling that such and such a person knows more than he is telling, or is likely to be useful to one, or whether it is the result of the ability which I luckily possessed of being able to tuck away bits of information in the back of one's mind and bring them out when they fitted some new bits of a puzzle. In any case I had a very strong feeling that I must get to know this man Rosenberg and must dig deeper into the whole German set-up, and that it was going to be important.

Just how important it was to be and how quickly it was to develop I did not then guess. Nor could one have guessed that a series of otherwise sane politicians could, in a few years, bury their heads so securely in the sands of domestic party politics as to land 'this England' into a second world war unready and unarmed—a war which was to disband the Empire and leave us beggared and bewildered. Yes, considerable absence of clear thinking, as my Chief would say.

As I saw Bill and Rosenberg off in the murk of Liverpool Street Station on a foggy day, Rosenberg promised that as soon

as the Party was firmly in the saddle I should be one of the first
Englishmen to come over to Berlin and meet and talk with
Hitler and see the set-up of the National Socialist movement for
myself, and, with one of his few smiles, he promised the station
would be nice and clean for me.

Had Rosenberg confined his visits to London to this first one
he would not, I think, have attracted the ridicule and abuse he
got when he came back a few years later under the aegis of
Ribbentrop. A badly publicised visit to the Astor home at
Cliveden and a wreath placed at the Cenotaph were about the
worst public relations that could have been thought up. No
doubt Rosenberg, acting on Hitler's instructions, thought he
could get *The Times* articles toned down by direct approach to
the Astors. It is possible that Ribbentrop was trying to damage
Rosenberg's reputation in Berlin; there was little love lost between
them and Ribbentrop continually resented Rosenberg's closeness
to Hitler and also Bill's position as unofficial adviser on England's
reactions.

Perhaps because of his first visit to London and what seemed
to be a genuine liking by the man for both Bill and me we formed
a strange kind of relationship with this fellow and, although nearly
all the ideas of the National Socialists were completely repugnant
to an ordinary Englishman, there was some strange fascination in
seeing them put into practice with such little delay, a state of
affairs which would be impossible in a parliamentary democracy.
It was like having a nightmare and then watching it come true
relentlessly—little use to ignore it and pretend it would never
happen.

The rise of Hitler to become Chancellor during the years 1931
to 1933 is history. William de Ropp was keeping me well informed
of such political aims and objectives as fell from the lips of Rosenberg and, latterly, Hitler himself. In fact, so well did Bill play his
part that he was taken on by Rosenberg as his 'English Agent'. By
1933 there was definite information that Hitler was flouting the
Versailles Treaty and starting openly to build and train a new
German Air Force. The Air Staff naturally wanted to know
what was going on. I had been able to recruit one or two

useful sources of information in Europe but Germany was
still elusive.

Ken Bartlett was the chief of the overseas sales branch of the
Bristol Aircraft Company, makers of some of the finest aircraft
and aero engines in the world. He was also a friend of mine.
We cooked up the idea that if we made de Ropp the Bristol agent
in Berlin, and if he in turn could suggest to Rosenberg that
Britain might be ready to agree to manufacture by Germany of
the latest (not quite) Bristol engines still on the secret list, the
bait might let Bartlett into the circle of German aviation specia-
lists. We argued that if they turned down the offer they must be
very confident of their own superiority, and that if they showed
interest we should only be disclosing our second best.

I got the Air Ministry technical branch to play along and I
think the best evidence of our success comes from the published
diaries of Rosenberg himself.*

14th May, 1934

Captain Bartlett from the Bristol aero-engine works has come with
a letter of introduction from Geschwaderführer Winterbotham of
the Air Ministry. He wants to install the new and still secret motor
here, emphasising that this is the first time the Ministry has given
him a letter of introduction. I ordered Obermüller to give him a
luncheon at which the chief designers of the Army, Navy and Air
Ministry were present. Thus the success of eighteen months' work has
become obvious, since the British Air Staff has officially given its
permission to complete the German air-defence.

In 1934 Rosenberg, true to his word, invited me to visit Berlin
and see for myself what National Socialism was all about. The
story of my activities from 1933 to 1938 is very much the story
of the rise of Nazi Germany and the rebirth of her mighty armed
forces, and although the greater part which deals with that
period is told in a lighter vein, consistent with the character
I assumed for my association with the Nazi 'Top Boys',
the underlying theme was in deadly earnest: on the one
hand the desperate efforts made by the Nazis by cajolery
and fear to keep Britain out of World War Two; on the

*Das Politische Tagebuch Alfred Rosenbergs, Musterschmidt-Verlag, 1956.

other hand determination to find out exactly what we should be up against if and when that war came.

My cover was good. I was listed in the Air Force list as a member of the Air Staff. I had a small office in the Air Ministry at Adastral House, mostly full of other people's filing cabinets, and I took care to be seen there often. I knew that if I was to mix with the top Nazis discreet enquiries would be made in London. They were; as a result of the success of Rosenberg's visit to London I decided to assume the character of one who was both interested in and even mildly enthusiastic about the 'new Germany'. It would be easy to be interested, not so easy to be enthusiastic; nevertheless, I would have to play it coolly in order to draw out my informants to the limit. I had done my homework on the Nazi political set-up and was ready to go.

3

Hitler

The *Reichstag* had gone up in flames. There was much speculation as to whether the Nazis had burnt it down in order to give themselves the opportunity to take complete control of government. They did seize the opportunity but Rosenberg told me, I believe quite truthfully, that they did not plan the fire and that it was in fact the Bulgarian Communist who was caught in the act who started it; nevertheless, it was too good an opportunity to miss.

Rosenberg himself was a member of the *Reichstag* before the fire. I felt he took a delight in showing me the blackened ruins; apparently he had once been ejected from his seat personally by the then Jewish Chief of Police. He never forgot or forgave.

It is possible that the Russians, who took the Nazi movement much more seriously than we did, got one of their sympathisers to do the burning in the hope that the reaction of the German people would be to turn on this new Nazi menace and destroy it. Whatever the truth, the fire worked for Hitler—the Nazis took over complete administration of the country.

There was no excuse for the mild surprise of His Majesty's Government. The writing was on all the walls, illuminated by the swastika. It was not in diplomatic language and it was apparently deemed prudent not to read it.

Hitler had written his book, *Mein Kampf*, while he had been in prison as a result of his early revolutionary activities in Munich. It was a militant book setting out the beliefs and principles of the Nazi dictatorship and, with its promises of military conquest, it was designed to get the support of the army, a very necessary ally in any political coup. I was therefore able to brief myself about the aims of the new movement before going to see the author

30

of the book. Bill had also given me a pretty good idea of what to expect.

After he had been in power for some years Hitler is reputed to have written a sequel which, if it ever existed, was never published. Rosenberg referred to it once; I never saw it, but I can guess at some of the changes he made to the original version. It would, I feel sure, have emphasised more strongly his hatred of the Communists and probably pinpointed the necessity for recasting the military priorities, with a greater bias to the East than the West. It would also have emphasised the proper place of the Army in the National Socialist state.

There was, in 1934, no scheduled air service so it was a question of the sea and rail route. This was, however, the only time I had to use the slower method; afterwards, I would have a free seat on one of the Lufthansa JU 52's, those aircraft that looked as if they were made of corrugated iron, sturdy horses which could and did become war-horses overnight.

I had been given a compartment to myself and no doubt the guard had been instructed to see I was not disturbed. What attractively coloured head-gear the German Railway officials wear. My mind went back to an unpleasant night in the bitter cold of January in 1919 when, as prisoners-of-war, we were huddled in our train at Frankfurt-on-Oder on our way to repatriation. Someone who didn't like us had connected up the coaches to the gas used for lighting and in the dark turned on the taps. A broken window just saved the night and all hell was let loose.

Now an elderly Jewish woman came into my compartment. She talked a little while to try to find out what I was doing as an evident V.I.P. on my way to Berlin. She shrewdly summed up my inquisitive nature and with, I imagine, considerable risk to herself warned me of the evil intentions of Hitler and his men. I gathered she was the wife of a publisher in Berlin and had been to England to make arrangements for her family to leave Germany without delay. She was lucky and wise.

I became sadder and more puzzled as I went back and forth to Germany in the following years why the Jewish people in Germany, with all their intelligence and ingenuity, appeared

31

incapable of foreseeing what was in store for them. There seemed to be a paralysis of mind and a feeling it could never really happen.

Perhaps they hoped for some strong foreign intervention, or some reaction from the army. Perhaps they and others overseas underestimated the number of adherents to this new Nazi movement. They should not have done. I, as a newcomer to the scene, was soon to see for myself the swing to National Socialism as the Brown Shirts came out like ants from a nest—tall ones, short ones, fat ones, thin ones, bearded ones, middle-aged and young ones. Perhaps it was because this odd collection in uniform was so unlike the popular conception of an organised army that its political strength was at first underestimated.

As the overnight train from Holland drew into Berlin on a fine February morning in 1934 I was totally unprepared for my reception. Evidently all the other passengers had been warned to stay in their compartments and as the train moved slowly along an almost empty platform my coach came to a halt, with all the precision of the V.I.P. trains at Victoria Station, right opposite a real red carpet, the first and only time I have had one for my exclusive use. As I stepped down, a little bewildered, there was Rosenberg in immaculate Nazi uniform, rather self-conscious and evidently wondering what my reactions would be. Bill was doing his best to stop laughing. To the railway officials and Rosenberg's bodyguard the whole thing was deadly serious. A *Heil Hitler* salute, a welcoming handshake, a few words of greeting, the click of many heels, and Nazi Movement Drill Number One went into immediate action.

This was the first time that I had encountered it, but I was to do so many times in those early days of the 'revolution'. You turn sharply in the direction of your car or your hotel, or wherever you are making for and you do a half-walk, half-run for it. You jump into your car, the engine of which is already running, you clutch whatever you can to prevent yourself making an undignified backward somersault as the car jumps away. I just caught sight of the bodyguard jumping into the second black Mercedes and we were off, two minutes flat from the time I stepped from the train until we were speeding along the broad street! My first thought was: 'What a waste of my one and only red carpet.' I had hardly had time to savour the situation before we were gone.

Travelling by Mercedes motorcade has its points; you get there quickly. The white buses, together with other traffic, had pulled dutifully into the kerb, the brown-shirted supporters on the pavement halted, faced the road and shot out their arms in a *Heil Hitler* salute, and the be-swastika'd policeman swells with a new-found importance as he waves you across the inter-section. The reason for the rapid movement drill was that ever since the Munich marchers had been shot up by the police the top boys of the Movement had taken care not to be picked off. So the drill was established. At least it makes you pick your feet up when running up hotel steps. I have seen even Goering doing it, surprisingly lightly for a man of his size. These tactics, like the interminable *Heil Hitler* salutes, were eased off gradually as the regime became stabilised, but the habit died hard, even up to 1936.

In 1934 the *Heil Hitler* salute was one of the most extraordinary sights I have ever witnessed. Whenever one went out in the streets of Berlin, the whole population seemed to be greeting each other with this extraordinary gesture. It was like a chorus dance in a Hollywood musical, and from the looks on their faces many of the more elderly citizens treated it as such; but it served its purpose, as a bolster to the pride of those who bulged a bit in their uniforms, and as propaganda and a sign of togetherness so beloved of the German race—that desire to be a crowd by people who are not quite sure of themselves.

I was to stay with Bill and his wife in their flat on the Kurfurstendamm; luckily the flat was fairly high up and looked out over the back. Kurfurstendamm was, and I believe again is, the gayest street of Berlin, a bit noisy both by day and by night. How different were the square rooftops in Berlin from the old crazy ones of Paris and the dingy rows of slated gables of London. Rooftops have a lot of character.

Funny, too, how white the buses and trams seemed. Some of the more blasé travellers tell me the only way they can remember where they are is by the colour of the buses—red for London,

c

green for Paris and New York, white for Berlin, etc. I used to
find the language a safer guide.

Bill's flat was very comfortable. I wanted to sit down and take
in the situation; I simply had to get rid of the feeling I was just
another member of some comic opera. Also I had to brief myself
on my visit: Whom should I meet? Where should I be going?
What must be avoided? It is vitally necessary to do one's homework on these occasions. I was in for a busy week, especially as I
wanted to see something of Berlin while I was there. Although
Jimmy was an excellent cook our usual daily round was breakfast
in the flat, with other meals when and where we could take them.
Time seemed to mean very little to the very busy leaders of the
New Germany, and I did not want to miss any chance of meeting
people who could help me to estimate the new regime.

A good many people have told of their first meetings with
Hitler. To many, no doubt, it was just an amusing experience—
made a good story. To me it was important. I now knew this man
was going to matter, not just to me but to all that I cared for. I
must get to know him and to know how he thought. Could I
make a success of our meeting? If so, it would undoubtedly help
Rosenberg to help Bill to help me.

Unlike some of Hitler's other visitors I had no official or
parliamentary status to maintain. I had no false dignity to
preserve or over-sized self-importance to be wounded. In the
event I had only an intense desire to laugh, not from any nervousness, but merely because the whole set-up was just *too* fantastic
for words.

It was the morning after my V.I.P. arrival. I had travelled light,
just a grey flannel suit and a toothbrush. Bill put on a new bow
tie, a blue one to match his eyes and 'accentuate the Aryan', as
he put it, and we got a taxi direct to Rosenberg's office. Berlin was
looking quite gay; the cafés in the Tiergarten were getting set for
their morning customers; the bright scarlet of the Nazi banners
gave more than a touch of colour. By contrast Rosenberg's office
was rather drab, considering his position; no vast rooms with
polished floors but nevertheless workmanlike. From here we
boarded the now familiar motorcade en route for the Chancellory

where, true to form, we galloped out of the cars, up the steps, straight into Alice's Looking-Glass Land.

Here in the great hall with its vast floor of large black and white marble squares were neatly arranged a score of tall figures in faultless black uniforms, their white gloved hands resting on the guns on either side of their belts. Each was standing stiffly to attention on his allotted white marble square. The illusion was startling and as a Black Pawn stepped smartly forward to inspect the party I fully expected the Red Queen to come skipping down the great stairway. The black pawns also extended up the stairs, one on either side every three steps, and as I followed up behind Rosenberg I had the new experience of being visually, if not physically, frisked. I got used to it after a while.

By the time I reached the head of the stairs I had a feeling, so tense were these gentlemen in black, that had I not been six-foot tall, with blue eyes and fair hair, I should have been bundled off to some distant dungeon. The whole atmosphere was so different from anything I had known before; not even the prison camps of World War One had the same sinister aura of ruthlessly efficient security. Of course, the whole set-up was also meant to impress the visitors, especially the German ones.

We had to wait a little while in the red plush ante-room. Rosenberg was silent and, I think, a little nervous as to what sort of impression I should make on his Führer, and also because we were being kept waiting rather a long time. Apparently the gentleman responsible for producing the plans for the whole new network of autobahns across Germany was in with Hitler at the time. As he emerged from the guarded double doors his grin was the measure of his success. He had got the go-ahead and was almost incoherent with excitement that his plans had got his beloved Führer's blessing.

Within five years I was to see the results of that interview in the shape of completed motorways; each straight as a die for five miles, then a slight turn, in order, as he put it, to keep the drivers awake. (Shades of our Minister of Transport arguing it out with about three hundred and fifty different local authorities over some three years before any action can start!)

The moment had now arrived and I was almost propelled

through the doors—I fancy it was a last attempt by the black guards to frisk me since, as a guest of Rosenberg, they had not quite dared to do so before.

It was a lovely room, in the old Chancellory. Tall windows, with blue brocade curtains, cast a sunny glow on some twenty yards of polished, honey-coloured wood floor; tapestries hung on one wall and, right at the other end, behind a vast desk—I think it was of French design—sat a little man, forelock, moustache and all. He was dressed in the simple brown shirt and black tie, with nothing on this uniform except the swastika armband to proclaim him the new Prophet.

The scene was much as I had been led to expect; fantastic, nevertheless; and I managed to keep my face straight whilst doing the long walk. When I arrived at the other end, however, the musical-comedy setting was almost too much for me. Fortunately, remembering Lord Chesterfield's advice to his son on the subject of public laughter, I broke only into a wide smile.

This seemed to amuse Hitler. He stood up, out shot a hand, not in the now familiar salute but to be shaken in the ordinary way. He, too, was smiling. What extraordinary eyes he had—they seemed to be protruding almost out of his head. Many people have commented on the hypnotic quality of his eyes; to me they were just very fishy, reminding me of a dead blue-eyed cod! His complexion was too pink and white but this was, I think, due to his time spent both in prison and now in his office for most of the daylight hours. Later, as he got out and about more, he developed a more healthy tan.

Neither of us spoke; I think I was too busy studying the Little Man; he was certainly weighing me up. Then Rosenberg and Bill, who had remained at the other end of the room, came up smiling and everybody started talking at once.

It struck me again how nervous Rosenberg had been as to whether I should hit it off with his master. I learned later that Hitler liked tall people and as I looked unmistakably Aryan and somewhat informal in grey flannels, I was evidently a success. It was immediately obvious that Hitler and Rosenberg were very close friends indeed and that Bill was right in the party too. Hair was now definitely down! Hitler suggested we move to a small round table some fifteen yards away—it was the only other piece of furniture in the room, anyway, barring a few chairs. We sat down and talked.

Hitler seemed to have a soft spot for airmen; I suppose, having been an infantry corporal in World War One, there was still some glamour attached to the *fliegers*, those men who, as he described it, were the last to know the individual chivalry of war. Anyway, we talked about World War One, and the fact that I had been shot down by Goering's bunch and was in no way bitter about my eighteen months as a prisoner-of-war pleased him. His voice was low and the harshness of Berlinese gently rounded by his Austrian origin. We talked as people who had shared a war talk in clubs and bars the world over. He was a perfectly normal, relaxed human-being chatting about old times and being skilfully led on by Bill to talk of the present.

Yes, he too believed in the strange comradeship of the air and he hoped I would find the lads of his new air force as good as the old ones. Oh, yes, the German Air Force was coming along nicely. The young men could now abandon their gliding exercises and get down to real flying training. He went on to tell me the latest figures of aircraft and squadrons. He was well briefed and proud of it and obviously enjoyed talking quite freely; I wondered why.

Now, the Germans, under that ill-wrought document, the Versailles Treaty, were not allowed an air force. Up to the time of the Nazis they had had to confine their activities to gliding. The General Staff had managed secretly to train a few pilots in Russia but the completely open defiance of the Treaty was a new line and a pointer to what was to come. Hitler was very well-informed about his new air force and as many of the details fitted in with what I already knew there was no reason to doubt the remainder.

Here, then, was the first open challenge to the Versailles Powers. What would His Majesty's Government do about it and why had Hitler been so completely frank? The answers to these two questions, which appear from time to time in these pages, give the clue to the policy of the Nazis towards the United Kingdom and of the British Government towards its own people during those fateful years 1935–39.

For the moment I had not worked this thing out. I was glad

enough to get confirmation from the Number One Nazi of information I was receiving from other sources concerning the present and future strength of the German Air Force. It would, I hoped, help me to convince our own government of this menace; I was a bit innocent and, of course, was not aware at this time of the Cabinet's policy towards it. Hitler had firmly confirmed the figure of some five hundred first line aircraft in squadrons by the end of 1934.

He had about talked himself out on the subject of air forces—I had better switch to something else. So I asked him what his personal reactions were towards the Communists. At this he became transfigured; his colours came up; with fishy eyes sparkling, he rose to his feet and there, in the great room, his now high-pitched staccato voice echoing round the walls, he addressed not three but three thousand people. It was stupendous, colossal, all-colour wide-screen stuff!

Again I had an irresistible desire to laugh, though this was long before Charlie Chaplin had made such a shattering comedy of the whole business. Again I managed instead to smile just as Hitler was delivering one of those twenty-words-all-joined-together pieces of Teutonic vituperation. In a flash he stopped, his bulging eyes returned to their sockets, he caught my eye, actually laughed and sat down. Somewhere this little Austrian had got a sense of humour; would that he had retained it. He must have been the only one of that outfit with the ability to laugh at himself.

Having had our bit of fun with Communism, Hitler now turned to what seemed to me to be his other pet theme and one that he obviously wanted to put across to the British Government. Multiplicity of authority was, of course, anathema to a dictator and Hitler now told me quietly and with a natural conviction how he and his colleagues believed that unless something drastic was done, sometime in the not far distant future dozens of small black, white, yellow and khaki states would be pursuing an entirely nationalistic policy and everybody would be trying to order the world to their own particular advantage with the resultant chaos and risk of wars. This would obviously be intolerable.

'There should,' said Hitler, 'be only three major powers in the world; the British Empire (as it then was), the Americas, and the Germanic Empire of the future.' This latter would include Europe and 'all the lands to the East'. In this way no single power would be able to dominate the others; England, with one or two exceptions, should continue her role in Africa, and Germany would take care of Russia, China and the Far East. All questions of economic, material and cultural improvement could be much more easily and quickly resolved between three great powers. It was as simple as that.

His parting words were to become much more significant later. He was sorry, he said, that England had not been able to give him some form of support, however small; as a result he had had to *'sell half his birthright to the Army'*.

It had been a crowded hour with one of his most significant pieces of information coming right at the end. With a friendly smile we shook hands. As we left a tall, rather gaunt man in a lounge suit tried to get my name, rank and number, but was politely told by Rosenberg to mind his own business. This was a type called *Hangstaffel*, a hanger-on, who had got himself a job as a sort of Public Relations officer with the foreign press. Obviously, if I was with Bill I must be some sort of press-wallah, and what was I doing seeing his precious boss without his knowledge? At least, this was the gist of Rosenberg's comments. No love lost there, evidently, but it was a pointer to the duplication of jobs which set up pockets of jealousy in the Party.

I met Hitler again several times and saw him on a number of occasions before the end of 1937, but only once again did I see the same sense of fun on his face. It was several years later and he was now the undisputed Führer of the Reich. Ribbentrop, who disliked both Rosenberg—the dislike was mutual—and Bill, was now Foreign Secretary. The old informal meetings were out but Bill and I had been invited by Ribbentrop to a very official reception. It was just prior to one of those Nuremberg Rallies. Berlin was full of foreign princes and politicians who, even if they did not intend to jump on the band-wagon, were preparing to play it both ways. The American diplomats and Press were being given the soft treatment and there were the usual adoring hangers-on, including starry-eyed Unity Mitford. Now all the guests were formed into a great circle ready to receive the imperial hand-shake.

I must say the Little Man did it very well. There was none of the strutting, heel-clicking, bending-in-the-middle nonsense so beloved by the military. He came quietly along, a rather cheesy smile beneath the absurd little moustache. Bill and I were standing together and as he shook hands the fixed smile broadened into a grin and, for a fleeting moment, the sparkle of fun came back into his eyes as he murmured: 'See how far I've come now.'

Ribbentrop had not been meant to hear what was said, nor had he done so; this was obviously an insult! He glared at both of us; we had obviously been invited to see Ribbentrop in all his glory! Bill began to chuckle and I thought it was time to make ourselves scarce. So full of intrigue was the whole atmosphere at that time, one could not help seeing and hearing little groups of people looking one over and discussing whom one could be.

Rosenberg had not been present; in fact, Ribbentrop had allowed nobody to spoil his triumphant presentation of his master. But we found Rosenberg having a beer at his favourite café not far from Bill's flat. He even raised a smile when we told him about the twitching wine-waiter, as Ribbentrop was unaffectionately called. He had a twitch of the face which was uncontrollable and had been a wine merchant in civil life. I never did discover how and why he eventually got the job as Ambassador to London.

A good example of the duplication of responsibilities which was so evident in high Nazi circles is the report made by Rosenberg to Hitler on 18th December, 1933, some two months before my first visit to Berlin.

> I was told that the German Air Ministry had made demands in such a blunt manner from the British Air Attaché in Berlin, that he felt obliged by his office to report these demands to London. Thus a plan of Germanophile circles has been baffled: the plan was to ask for our special friend from the English Air Staff, Major Winterbotham, as an Air Attaché. Nevertheless, without the knowledge of the German Embassy in London, they succeeded in getting a confidential person into the embassy of another mission, who was able now to give all the information. I let Baron de Ropp know, who passed it on directly to the Air Staff in London.*

*Musterschmidt-Verlag, 1956.

It is amusing to see how Rosenberg got his own back by informing us through de Ropp that the German Air Ministry had planted an agent in another embassy. It enabled us to plug the leak and, as no doubt Rosenberg calculated, sowed some seeds of mistrust regarding the sincerity of a supposedly friendly nation.

And now back to my first visit to Berlin.

Here was I, evidently being tried out by the top Nazis as a possible contact in their relations with the United Kingdom. Either from lack of diplomatic experience or from mistrust of official contacts they seemed to prefer the unorthodox approach through people like myself, with apparently no axe to grind. If I could put myself across it would open up endless possibilities for Bill and me to keep abreast of developments inside Nazi Germany.

I had, I think, made a reasonable impression on Hitler; he had, unexpectedly, made a reasonable impression on me. His two personalities, the quiet interesting talker, and the staccato-voiced rabble-rousing tub-thumper, could seemingly be switched on at will. Not even his small sense of humour could account for his absurd quiff and moustache. How did it come about that this little Austrian housepainter, who went through World War One as an infantry corporal on the Western Front, achieved the authority and the stature to lead a nation and finally the madness to alter the history of the world?

I knew him for only a few short years, 1934 to 1937, not well, but enough to see how each year took toll of his health and any joy he had in life. I saw his features grow sallow and puffy and his expression more troubled.

Rosenberg told me that when the movement first started in Munich, Hitler was the 'talker' of this strange band of rebels. At first they had little clear idea of what they wanted to do except change the existing order. One got the impression that if there had been a Hyde Park Corner in Germany, Hitler would have been there on his soap-box. One can visualise the rather undecisive authorities of the day saying 'That little trouble maker again.'

I gathered that it was only after this band of rebels had worked for some months on the ideas of Hess and Rosenberg that the basis of the new ideology began to emerge. 'The Blueprint for

Change', as Rosenberg called it, began to get around. Even the rebels were surprised at the number of supporters. As I have said, the climate was just right: Germany wanted a new hero.

In the early days and, in fact, even when I first met Hitler in 1934, he seemed to lean to some extent on his two closest friends, Hess and Rosenberg. His ability to hold an audience was one of his principal assets to this small group. Rosenberg described it as hypnotic; it may have been, though it did not hypnotise me, but I have seen a crowd of many thousands whipped up to a state bordering on mass hysteria by this extraordinary man.

Adversity is always supposed to bring out the best in a genius. There is little doubt that Hitler's imprisonment by the German government gave this small band of political rebels time to sort out their ideas and clarify them in book form—Hitler's *Mein Kampf* and Rosenberg's *The Myth of the Twentieth Century*.

There was some speculation abroad at first as to whether Hitler was just a puppet of his party. Personally, I don't think this was ever the case. Certainly he was probably chosen as their spokesman at the beginning owing to his gift of the gab, but there is no doubt in my own mind that he became their leader as of right.

Gradually he found stronger men, more used to action than dreaming up new philosophies, to support him, and with them he grew in power and authority, if not in wisdom. Alas, the stronger men who had jumped on the bandwagon began to pursue their own pet hates and theories. Streicher and Himmler got busy with the Jews; Hess got busy on the trade unions which he dissolved— maybe he saved post-war Germany from some of the crippling effects of over-antiquated prejudices in this field. Rosenberg was given a free hand to go ahead with his plans for an Aryan-cum-pagan Europe; Goering built himself an air force; von Schirach trained the whole youth of Germany to be fit to fight, also to be very fertile, and so on; but Hitler was now in full command.

Alas, with power came not so much corruption but megalomania. How very few mortals can take power. Generations of authority coupled with responsibility often bring justice and compassion, but it was hardly likely that Hitler and his henchmen could take it. Eventually the gods had their way. To anyone listening to Hitler during those final days in his Bunker in Berlin, ordering his long since disintegrated armies to new positions of defence on the Eastern Front, his madness and destruction were complete. And yet, if one sets aside for a moment all the more bestial activities of the Nazis, Hitler was the sole outspoken challenger of that time who foresaw the chaos, the trouble-making, intrigue and unrest the Communist countries would bring to a world divided by Iron and Bamboo Curtains' hatred and mistrust.

Tomorrow I was to meet Hess.

4

Hess, Rosenberg and Others

Hess, unlike his master, was ever content to be the shadow. He avoided the limelight and I think few people knew him intimately. His brown shirt also lacked any form of decoration but, like the rest of his clothes, was extremely well cut. His flaired breeches could not have been improved on by Savile Row; he was tall and slim, with a good leg for a boot; his boots were the envy of the Party. Not only were they real leather but they fitted him, and the shine on the black leather would have done justice to a cavalry batman. I could not make up my mind at first whether he was just shy of foreigners, not quite sure of himself, or just plain eccentric. He was certainly fastidious.

He had a very important job, that of Party Organiser, and did it extremely efficiently. He and Rosenberg were very close friends and it was evident now that there was, as Rosenberg had told me, an inner circle of friends—Hess, Rosenberg and Hitler, the originators of the ideas on which the thousand-year Reich was to be built. In due course Hess was nominated by Hitler as his Deputy.

The first time I met Hess was in his large plain but workman-like office in the Chancellory; nothing elaborate here, but the rows of hard benches facing his desk looked as if people came there to be told what to do. As I came up to say 'how-d'you-do', Hess struck a pose. He remained sitting, arms folded across his plain brown shirt, one beautifully shod leg thrust out beneath his large bare pinewood desk, his thick black eyebrows drawn down to a scowl. Was it because he did not want me to see his eyes that he stayed thus until I came right up to him. After all, I was an unknown Englishman and ought therefore to be properly impressed.

Hess, Rosenberg and Others

There was something odd about the Nazi uniform which I had never been able to pin down. Now, suddenly, I got it. In England, in the 'twenties or 'thirties, we were quite unused to anyone wearing just a soft shirt, buttoned up to the neck and down to the wrists, and accompanied by a black tie; open-necked, sleeves rolled up, yes. Perhaps it was my preoccupation with this uniform rather than his scowl which got him to his feet, or maybe it was my failure to click my heels or look in the least impressed with his pose. Anyway, he got up, actually smiled, and shook hands. I suppose they had to try on the big stuff in case someone expected it.

We got talking and the first thing I asked him was whether it was really necessary to dress up all their Party members in uniform. Hess did not try to bluff at all. He had obviously made a careful study of his fellow-countrymen and their psychology. He pointed out that 'in a bloodless revolution such as they had carried out it was necessary to have some visible solidarity. Also the Germans like a uniform; it gave them a sense of belonging to a group'. He went on to explain that the Germans, perhaps because they had not been colonisers like the British, were, as a people, not so self-reliant; uniform gave them a sense of togetherness.

I could, of course, have added that it gave some of them a good handle to do a bit of bullying and persuade others to join the movement; also, to strut, that inborn habit of many generations of conscripts. Uniform was also useful when it came to collecting money from the public. I am only glad the Germans did not adopt tassels bobbing in front of those little round peaked caps; already the very large round supporters looked odd enough, their shirts and breeches bulging at the seams.

I met Hess on several occasions during the 'thirties. I found a certain depth of character and level of intelligence which was often missing in other Nazi leaders. There was a latent sensitivity in place of the ruthless efficiency of the Goerings and the Himmlers. He certainly found more poise but always seemed diffident and retiring, and I doubt if he could have succeeded Hitler had things turned out differently for them. His flight to England during the war was quite in character. Despite his diffidence he had ample courage; he could see a little further ahead than his colleagues, and had seen the red light; he faced only a fifty-fifty chance of

45

survival and a ninety-nine-to-one chance against success, yet, nevertheless, he took the risk.

It was normal courtesy to call and make one's number at the British Embassy, especially as the Air Attaché was an old friend of mine. I also felt that I should give him the gist of my talk with Hitler; he was excited at my news. I told him I was going south with Rosenberg for a few days and would call and give him full details before I left Germany. Rosenberg was due to go down to Weimar for a Party get-together with the local area supporters. It was to be a three day trip with speeches and visits and he had asked Bill and me to go with him. I was anxious to see the new regime at work outside Berlin and also some of the country.

We set off next morning in Rosenberg's black Mercedes, thank goodness without any bodyguards. The road to Weimar passes through some very attractive country but it was strange to find how much of Germany is poor sandy soil, not much good from the point of view of agriculture; however, it grows good timber. Lunch off jugged hare and a bottle of hock in an old timbered pub at Wittenberg was served by a rather flustered landlord in traditional red waistcoat and white apron.

Rosenberg seemed more relaxed than in Berlin—the strain on life in the capital must have been very heavy in those early days. He had already lost some of the freshness I had seen in London. He had become dull and preoccupied much of the time; his complexion had become rather sallow, it was difficult to get him to smile—he was taking himself far too seriously—and only became lively when carried away by his own enthusiasm for some project such as the sterilisation of the unfit. After a few beers he would get morose—whether from tiredness or a touch of Chekhov, I don't know.

After lunch we strolled around the ancient town and as we looked up at the old church Rosenberg let me have a glimpse of one of the reasons for his atheism. 'You know,' he said, 'if we in Germany hadn't spent thirty years fighting amongst ourselves as to how we were supposed to say our prayers, you British wouldn't have had the chance to annex half the world.'

We had passed through the green valley of the Elbe, lazy in the wintry sun, into the hills and forests. How wonderfully kept the forests were, every tree straight and in apparently endless rows of weedless precision. Forestry is a great art in Germany and the State Foresters men of considerable importance in the society of the countryside; also, they have a uniform. I was complimenting Rosenberg on the tidy rows and the apparent absence of ill-formed trees and I inadvertently set him off on one of his pet subjects.

Not only were the trees to be all-perfect in Germany; the people, too, were to be subject to a strict genetic policy. Even then, only a short time after they had come to power, the Nazis had started on a policy of sterilisation; anyone who produced mongol or abnormal children would have to submit to sterilisation as a start.

After all, was not the Third Reich going to last for a thousand years, and we all know that long before that there wouldn't be enough food to go round. 'If the great Nordic races—and that includes the English'— said Rosenberg, 'are to survive, there will be no place for weaklings or fools. Is it not better to have a healthy, happy people by using such sciences as we have? Already, too, we are selecting true Nordic women for our experiments.'

Diabolical logic, perhaps; I had visions of studs of blue-eyed blondes! I have always believed that the difference between man and the other mammals was that the possession of a soul, or whatever you may wish to call it, gave man the right of freedom of choice, whether good or evil; but the Nordics were now to be treated like a vast herd of pedigree cattle in order that they might survive. This was 1934 and it was happening already.

Rosenberg had an excellent driver. He was a tall, rather Scottish-looking man of about thirty-five, with reddish hair and neat ginger moustache. He had been a racing driver before coming to Rosenberg, a thoroughly cheerful type who fed with us and smoked endless cigarettes, but despite his good handling of the car we did not arrive in Weimar until after dark.

It was raining but nothing was going to damp the ardour and enthusiasm of the local Nazis, and as the car slid up to the hotel steps the *heil*-ing became a roar. Here was a hero of the revolution come to Weimar and Weimar was going to show him what it

could do. The enthusiasm of the Party Members, many as yet
wearing only a scarlet swastika arm-band on their ordinary
clothes, the floodlights catching the brilliant colour of the be-
swastika'd banners hanging limply in the drizzle but forming a
solid canopy of crimson above the streets, seemed unreal but
somehow exciting.

No galloping into the hotel here. As I stood on the steps with
Rosenberg, my hand was shaken a hundred times by Party
Members of every conceivable shape and age, some crying with
emotion. It is just no good suggesting that National Socialism was
thrust upon the German people; the great majority swallowed it
hook, line and sinker.

We were already a little late but we managed to get a cold
snack before going along the street to the hall where a rally was
due to take place. I had no idea what to expect but the tension
and excitement were building up and I found it was rather
contagious; after all, this was my very first revolution as seen from
the top at close quarters. As we entered the great building—
Rosenberg, Bill, myself and two of the local big-wigs—the heads
of what must have been about five thousand people turned and
watched in silence as we made our way up the long aisle to the
front row of the stalls. In front of us again was a large amphitheatre, with tier upon tier of choristers, several hundred strong.
They were men of all ages, from the young and eager to the old,
moustached, bespectacled Teuton so familiar in our fairy stories.
On a small platform between the choir and the body of the hall
was a lectern from which Rosenberg would make his speech, but,
somehow, the eagle's wings had been elongated and spread out
to resemble the Nazi badge.

The whole audience and choir had risen as we came in. Now, as
we reached our seats, like a well-drilled battalion of sergeant-
majors they gave the *Heil Hitler* salute; arms shot out in front, one
just missing the top of my head from the row behind. Three times
they shouted as one man, down went the arms in silence. Despite
the hardness of the chairs, there was an odd feeling of unreality
about it all. I had discussed with Bill in Berlin the question of
giving the Nazi salute. I did not wish to embarrass Rosenberg;
on the other hand I certainly did not want to *Heil Hitler*. We

compromised by complying on this first occasion—we should probably have been lynched otherwise—but after my first visit, when the fervour had simmered down a bit, I stopped doing it. Never did I quite get what the choir was singing, the din was terrific, but I caught odd bits of Wagnerian crescendoes.

I think the story that Hitler had a collapsible spring support up his sleeve must really have been correct. I have seldom seen a more pathetic sight than when at the end of a rousing Nordic speech by Rosenberg the whole choir sang *Deutschland Uber Alles*, arms outstretched, starting just higher than the shoulder, but, alas, gradually sinking as the verse wore on. A sharp tap of the conductor's baton and up they all came again, only to subside slowly once more. Have you ever tried to sing with your arm outstretched level with your eyes for about ten minutes on end?

When the rally broke up Rosenberg, who had to talk to a great many people, handed me over to a bunch of young Nazis—cheery lads, proud of their ability to speak some English—and we all went off to the traditional beer-cellar. There must have been about a hundred odd, mostly young men, and I must say their high spirits were infectious. We talked no politics, the beer was good and flowing freely, when a waiter, with his eyes standing out on stalks, told me an Englishman wanted me on the telephone from Berlin.

I have found by experience that members of British embassies abroad, by virtue of their complete diplomatic immunity, attain a shattering sense of personal security, a state of affairs in no way automatically surrounding an ordinary United Kingdom citizen visiting countries with somewhat nervous governments. Perhaps that is why the Air Attaché on the other end of the phone, which I knew would be tapped, had no idea of the cold wave which went down my spine.

My friend in Berlin was as cheerful as ever; I am afraid I was icy. Apparently he had mentioned the first of my talks to the Ambassador, Sir Phipps, as the Germans called Sir Eric Phipps. He in turn demanded to see me at once so that he could telegraph my news to London. I supposed my friend had failed to tell him I was out of town for a few days; hence the summons back to Berlin. I pointed out that I was not subject to the whims of the Ambassador but would get back as soon as I could reasonably do so.

I expect I must have looked a shade too thoughtful as I returned to my drinking friends but I had to make up my mind quickly. Neither I nor Bill had any idea at that time how much use the Nazis thought we might be to them as unofficial links with London. Politically they could not take too long a shot. Rosenberg was coming over to my table. Bill was wisely staying away.

I took a quick decision which club to use to this hole. I explained to Rosenberg that, as *he* knew, my Government were a little cagey about individuals, especially ones with some sort of official connections like myself, coming to Germany at that time and I feared I was in for trouble with my superiors. (The Nazis knew me to be a 'liaison' officer in the Air Ministry List but had no idea of my real job.) How soon could he get me back to Berlin? I did not know whether he had swallowed my excuse; my companions certainly did; more beer all round and not to worry! Anyway, I bluffed it out until midnight, then went across to the hotel for bed.

Rosenberg, Bill and I each had a large room to ourselves next door to each other on the main floor, and soon after I had gone to bed, dead tired but fitfully awake, I heard a sound that took me back fifteen years—the measured tread of a sentry going up and down the passage outside my room. So this was it. Well, maybe I had better make the best of a comfortable bed while I could. Eventually I must have gone to sleep. I awoke to a knock on my door. It was Rosenberg; he was already dressed, and as he came over and sat by my bed he managed a fleeting smile.

I do not know how long he had been preparing his little speech, but as he sat there and quietly sympathised with me in my troubles with authority, he told me of the glories of defiance of the old order, of the splendid thing I was doing in standing up for the new. He personally would ask Hitler to see that no harm came to me for coming over to see him and his colleagues. I rather liked the man at that moment; he had rearranged his whole programme so that we could return to Berlin the following day. Ah well! now for breakfast. The sentry, by the way, had been to protect Rosenberg.

I spent most of that day looking around the old town of Weimar, which is to the Germans much the same as Stratford-on-Avon is to us and has the advantage of Goethe being the undoubted author of his works. Goethe's old timbered house had been turned into a delightful museum. On the walls were original Dürer drawings and the rooms were full of exquisite period furniture. Why worry about the Corps Diplomatique? I only hoped that my friend would not be overcome by more diplomatic madness and ring me up again from Berlin.

Next day we set out early on our way back. We had several calls to make on the way, the first at a school for Hitler Youth for boys of about nine to twelve years old. Owing to the change of time-table we arrived a day earlier than expected, and apparently no-one had warned the headmaster. Disaster! Everyone running in all directions. Rosenberg, quite unconcerned, led us into a large classroom, bare but for an enormous table in the middle, its foot-high sides holding in what seemed to be a large sand-pit. I thought, at first, that this was rather elementary stuff for these slightly older children. However, the teacher took one look at me and went beetroot; the kids, close-cropped, round-headed and brown-shirted, grinned at his discomfiture. One half of the school was learning how to attack a well-defended position held by the other side. The sand-pit was, in fact, a battlefield made up into hills and trenches and strong-points and so forth, and the battle was obviously at a critical stage.

There was only one thing for it; I volunteered to join in the game and brought a little air-warfare into play for the attackers. They were a cheery bunch of kids, poor little devils. Normality was now re-established and amidst a forest of *Heil Hitlers* we went on our way. But not very far. Our next call was to be at the House of Nietzsche and this, I now suspect, was one of the main reasons for Rosenberg's visit to Weimar.

I have never had the inclination to read much of this author's work, nor have I so far mentioned it in connection with the Nazi philosophy. I never expected to see what was going on here. It was a large house, steeply gabled, and stood well back behind dark pine woods. Inside were a massive pinewood staircase, doors and cornices, carved; the whole place had an overbearing rather than a pretentious air. A frail little old lady dressed in black, her pale blue eyes managing a proud smile, welcomed us in. This was

Frau Nietzsche, the author's widow. Beyond the hall, in a vast sombre book-lined library, were about twenty young men and women working like ferrets on the author's works. Apparently they were compiling some sort of anthology.

Rosenberg had first introduced himself to me as a doctor of Philosophy; no mention as to when he had got his degree, but he must at some time have read Nietzsche and from then on had begun to look upon himself as a minor prophet. I cannot help feeling from some of his rather unconnected utterances that he borrowed most of his 'philosophy' and strung it together to make up his Nazi religion of the great Aryan racial cult.

I got the impression, although I was not given the time to question any of the researchers, that there was some sort of basic Nazi philosophical work in preparation here. I wonder if the study was ever finished. Anyway, over a cup of coffee served from delicate Sèvres china off an incongruously massive carved pine-wood table, the little old lady talked to us of the days when Mussolini studied at her husband's knee and Hitler himself had been a frequent visitor. I wanted to ask if Lenin and Trotsky had passed that way.

My mind went back to a strange party on the terrace of a one-storey concrete block building not ten miles behind the German frontline on the fateful evening of Friday, 13th July, 1917.

I had miraculously survived a dog-fight between my own flight and about ten times as many members of the famous Richthofen Squadron. I had been shot down, engineless, rudderless, but still with my wings and one landing wheel, and now, by custom, I was being entertained by the men I had fought. The Moselle was cool and smooth—alas, I could not taste it due to a broken nose. The bemedalled young man who claimed my destruction was most reassuring: the war would soon be over. Only that week they had brought to Germany and sent on into Russia two men who would very soon close down the Eastern Front. Their names were Lenin and Trotsky. Little did they know what they were doing. Anyway, my informant did not have to worry; poor chap, he was killed soon after above the blood-bath of Passchendaele. . . .

The coffee was excellent. I only hope the old lady passed on before she had to face the Second World War. From all I heard about her husband she had a pretty tough life.

Rosenberg's driver made a good time on the misty road and I was thankful to get back with Bill to his cosy flat and the telephone. I still had to be careful but I managed to cool my friend's ardour considerably and agreed to come round and see Sir Phipps the next day. Jimmy had cooked a splendid meal so we spent that evening having a post-mortem on our not uneventful trip.

One thing seemed clear; the Nazis were quite happy about my passing on to the Embassy anything they had told me. Whether or not they believed my story about getting into trouble with my own authorities, I could, and no doubt would, be used as a useful channel to London. They must therefore want us to know about their rearmament programme. Why? This suited Bill and me. It would give us all the opportunities we needed to check and re-check their progress and their political objectives; also, I could check their information against other sources. The trip had also shown us the massive support for the Party—from the young with enthusiasm, from the old with the wisdom of self-preservation.

5

Reichenau on Russia

Back in Berlin a rather special lunch party had been arranged by Rosenberg. He wished me to meet Goering and 'some other friends', as he put it. The restaurant, with its dark oak panelling and red-plush decor, was so typically nineteenth-century German or English Victorian, the great table with its snow-white cloth bearing up manfully beneath the heavy array of silver and shining glass. The food was delicious and the hock superb. There was something, too, very special about the traditional German waiter in breeches, red waistcoat and apron. The room, the decor, and the waiters all added up. It was here that cabinet ministers, generals, and even royalty, had been wont to feed.

I was just wondering how I should react to the great swash-buckler himself, whom I had not yet met, when two young officers in civilian dress arrived and excused the great man; he had other important things to do. The two men were introduced to me, one, a Captain Wenninger, and the other, a Captain Kesselring. Neither spoke much English, or at least, would not admit to it.

Now, the Germans published every year a list of the officers filling the various appointments at their War Office. We do the same, I used to study this book carefully and I had noticed that, by 1934 each department of the German War Office had had an 'attached' officer added to its staff. One of the names rang a bell from my World War One flying days. Careful examination then showed that these attached officers were, in fact, all ex-Air Force officers. There was little doubt in my own mind that this was an Air Staff in training, camouflaged in the German War Office until the day when Goering's new Air Ministry would be built and the new

German Air Force launched upon the world; at that time it was still officially non-existent.

Wenninger and Kesselring were two of these officers. Both were, I should guess, around the forty mark, Wenninger perhaps the older. He was tall, fair and slim, with pleasant manners and a wide mouth which could smile, and, from what I could judge, not too many brains. His short black coat and striped trousers fitted him and looked natural. It struck me that these two had not quite known what to wear; they could not correctly wear German Air Force uniform, and so what? Kesselring was a different kettle of fish. He was square, swarthy, with beetling black eyebrows, and a taciturn, almost rude manner, and he made it quite obvious why his ill-fitting coat and trousers, which had very broad black and grey stripes and were evidently borrowed for the occasion, irked the man, who was not happy out of uniform. I have met his type in many countries and, indeed, in many walks of life— the sort who was going to get to the top, over whose back it did not matter.

The other guest at the lunch, General von Reichenau, arrived shortly after. Knowing the Army-Nazi tension, I was a little surprised but, judging by the enthusiasm with which Rosenberg introduced him, it was obvious that he was a Hitler man and a Nazi capture. Rosenberg stressed his friendliness to the Nazi cause. Reichenau carried through the brilliant stroke of making every army officer and conscript take a personal oath of allegiance to Hitler. The soldiers took this oath seriously; it further weakened the authority of the General Staff vis-a-vis the Nazis. He was a tall, typical, eye-glassed, slightly balding, duel-scarred, square-headed general of the High Command; there was only a small crease in his immaculate green uniform where he habitually bent at the waist on introduction; a good linguist, fluent in English, and, I guessed, in Russian, too; a brilliant and ambitious man, also a brave one; an amusing and informative conversationalist.

I discovered that there were several reasons for this lunch, which started rather formally. The two German Air Force officers were quite silent, evidently ordered to take their cue from the general. It was a little embarrassing to see Rosenberg, our host, solid and a bit inarticulate, having to rely on the vivacious general to get the party going.

It was about this time that His Majesty's Government was putting forward one of its well-meaning but impractical ideas about aeroplanes: the proposal was to ban the construction of bombers. I think everybody who knew anything about aeroplanes realised that even if some such agreement could ever be reached it could never achieve its object so long as civil aircraft had to be built, especially because at this stage of aeronautical development the two were virtually interchangeable. The Germans themselves had such a dual-purpose aeroplane at this time, the old 'tin-box', or the JU 52. This three-engined aeroplane was the basic civil air-liner of the Lufthansa (the German civil airline) in the 'thirties, and many hundreds of miles I flew in them; a good, sturdy sort of air transport which could become a bomber overnight. The baggage compartment was the correct size for bomb-racks; it had doors which opened downward and was at the centre of gravity.

On every flight, especially to England, two trainee German Air Force pilots were carried and it was often obvious when they took over the controls. These lads made no bones about it and they often used to come back into the cabin for a chat when they knew I was on board.

However, the camouflaged German Air Staff were evidently not quite sure how far the British Government was prepared to go in this matter, and whether the replacement of the JU 52 would also have to be a bomber-cum-civil aeroplane. So I was casually asked: 'Did I think the bomber could ever be internationally forbidden?' The answer was simple, if non-committal: 'So long as civil aeroplanes like the JU 52 could carry bombs, no-one could prevent construction of aeroplanes capable of conversion into bombers.'

Having got Item Number One off the list, with a nod to the two young men across the table—a nod which to me plainly said: 'Now you've got your answer; now, *I'm* going to talk about the Army;'—the General became even more affable and animated. Hardly noticing the very excellent food and wine, he told me in some detail how the Army was going to invade Russia.

This, in the middle 'thirties, was rather astonishing. Admittedly, one was prepared to hear all about the wonderful armaments of the new German Army, this was all part of the intimidation 'act'; but these disclosures of invasion strategy against the U.S.S.R. were of a different category, albeit evidently directed towards the same end. I knew that the Nazi hatred of the U.S.S.R. must come to a head sometime, but here was the whole thing on a plate.

The Nazis, who themselves were daily gaining experience in the battle for men's minds, saw at much closer quarters than ourselves the massacres and tyranny of Communism and could never understand why we, too, did not get red in the face at the mention of the word. They felt, I am sure, that we would surely welcome the destruction of the Bolsheviks. On the other hand, the High Command of the Army had been rather friendly with the Russian Generals before the Nazis came on the scene and this may have had something to do with their original dislike of Hitler's insistence on the march against Russia.

No wonder the Nazis were pleased with Reichenau who had fallen in with their views and, in fact, was now so enthusiastic about it he forsook the excellent Charlotte Russe to expand once more on his plans for conquest. Quite apart from his unquenchable enthusiasm for his job, I felt that the message he was putting across was that Germany alone would fight and destroy the common enemy, Communism, if Great Britain would just keep out of it all. Bill was not surprised at all this: Hitler had told him of his intention to invade the U.S.S.R. as far back as 1932. Now the planning was evidently well under way.

From his conversation I gathered that Reichenau was planner-in-chief for the Southern Front; he was also destined to be Chief-of-Staff of the Southern Army Group. As he talked and unfolded his plans, his confidence in success was supreme. I think he forgot for a while the real reason for this lecture and found it immense fun to be able to tell someone about it. I cannot, alas, repeat word for word this amazing lecture but I will try and give the gist of it. The techniques seemed to apply not only to Russia.

The new Army technique was to use speed as the primary factor in every movement; all troops would travel light in fast troop-carriers to keep up with the armoured divisions which would thunder ahead non-stop. In this way the country won would be immediately consolidated. All baggage, ammunition, and hot meals would come up separately by fast motor echelons and by air. The Russians would be bewildered; and much more besides. The northern, central and southern thrusts would divide and destroy the defending armies; speed, speed and more speed, the armoured tanks forming a spear-head. The mistake that others had made was not being able to follow up the tanks with infantry. Now all that would be remedied; the infantry would be right there behind the tanks; they would conquer at the rate of two hundred miles a day.

I asked him how this plan would work in a Russian winter. He said there would not be a Russian winter; it would be 'a German one, with everybody nicely ensconced in warm houses'. Other people have made the same mistake but his talk, which spun on for the best part of an hour, did give a clue to the sort of warfare the Germans had in mind. Already I knew that their Air Force was planning for maximum mobility by divorcing the maintenance and supply side of their squadrons from the operational, one of their greatest mistakes.

In fact, so sure were they of quick success that no repair organisation was created until well on in the war, the theory being that all damaged aircraft would simply be scrapped and replaced by new ones, and that all aerodrome service and maintenance would be done by a separate organisation; a squadron would simply have its pilots and its aircraft to fly from one place to another. This is all very well so long as the supply of new aeroplanes keeps pace with casualties, which, of course, it did not, and the failure was one reason why the Luftwaffe could not keep up its blitz on England in 1940. Another was the fact that so sure were they that England would not fight that their Messerschmitt fighters were built with a very limited fuel range, and when it came to escorting bombers over England they could not stay long enough in the air to do the job properly.

The younger Air Force officers did not take much part in Reichenau's extravaganza. Evidently air supply would be one of the principal functions of the German Air Force on the Eastern

Front. I asked if they were worried about Russian fighters; no, they didn't worry at all. Here they were probably right. The much publicised Russian Air Force never really made the grade. The whole German plan obviously depended on speed and a disorganised resistance. How well this blitzkreig strategy worked in France we found out to our cost, but the Russians were able to go back to the Volga as fast as Reichenau could follow them and there, when the Germans were fully extended, they stood and fought. Reichenau, I think, had not allowed for this. He finally shot himself in a railway carriage on the Eastern Front, in the middle of a Russian winter.

The final surprise of the lunch was still to come. As we all got to our feet, very full of good food, the General, face glistening, was still able to bend in the middle as he took his leave. Rosenberg asked me 'which of the two young Air Force officers would make the best air attaché for London.' 'He would have to be technically for civil aviation, but this would fool nobody,' Rosenberg said wryly.

Despite the fact that neither of them had uttered more than a few words it was an easy choice to make. Wenninger, with his amiable grin, was unlikely to cause any unpleasantness or to learn very much. I later discovered, when he got to London, that his wife was a cousin of Ribbentrop. She was a commanding personality and had poor Wenninger well under her thumb. Kesselring was a very different type, as we learned later. I think he silently thanked me for passing him up. We met again in 1937; by then he was a colonel and very friendly, for him, and offered to fly me back to Berlin from Nuremberg. He was, incidentally, an excellent pilot. Bill took advantage of the offer as I had to return to Paris.

Next time Kesselring crossed my path he did not know it was mine and the story properly belongs to the chapter on my clandestine high-altitude photographic spy planes. We all came up against Kesselring, of course, many times during the war when, as a field-marshal, he was later in supreme command of the Mediterranean theatre of war. I was glad to know where Kesselring was and what he was doing. I had rightly judged him as the rough, tough, bludgeoning type of Prussian, ever determined to

59

get to the top at whatever cost, but totally bereft of imagination. I watched him make one mistake after another in the Mediterranean campaign. His reactions became almost predictable, which was a considerable advantage to the Allies. I was also able to give Oliver Stanley, at that time running the enemy deception unit, a tip or two which may have helped them to fool Kesselring so completely concerning our Sicilian landing in 1943. There is no doubt he swallowed completely the bait of the drowned messenger off Portugal.

Wenninger duly arrived in London, bringing with him a number of bottles of wild raspberry liqueur which he knew I had enjoyed in Germany. I think Rosenberg must have put him up to it. It is really an Alsatian drink but in Germany I found it a useful alternative to the rather heavy, sickly liqueurs which Rosenberg himself seemed to fancy. Wenninger's tour of duty was quite harmless, I am sure; he was charming and quite ineffective.

The one thing which we did not wish the Germans to learn about was our radar, and the fact that at the beginning of the war they had no idea what we were up to is a measure of our success.

Rosenberg's Diary of 14th May, 1934, gives his account of my visit.

Major Winterbotham was here 'on vacation' from the 27th February up to the 6th March. Then I arranged for him to meet Reichenau, Loerzer, Hess, two commodores, and finally Hitler. Major Winterbotham conveyed the greetings of the British airmen. The Führer said that the Air Force had been the truly knightly weapon of the World War. As for the rest, the English have been a dangerous enemy because Germany was forced to keep two-thirds of her aeroplanes on the English frontline. Moving to present times, the Führer gave expression to his conviction that no doubt the French were superior in numbers of aircraft but he considered the English stronger in value. As for the rest, he might be in favour of considerable reinforcement of the English Air Force, primarily for the following reason: that he was to demand for the defence of Germany a certain percentage in relation to the fleets of our neighbouring states. Now this necessary percentage was approaching the British numerical strength, a fact he did mind very much, because various inferences would be drawn from it; England could have twice as many aircraft and even more, this would be only welcome.

The conversation took a satisfactory course and Winterbotham made a brilliant report in London. I went to Weimar with Winterbotham and de Ropp, to show him the style of our meetings. I showed him the Goethe-Haus, the Nietzsche-Archives; then coffee with the eighty-year-old Frau Foerster-Nietzsche, who had an astonishingly vivid mind; then we visited our school in Eggendorf, where the burgomasters of Thüringen, together with jurists, etc., have courses. There was a short address on the duty of ideological training. All these things, especially the frame of mind in Germany, deeply impressed Winterbotham; everything was so far from any propaganda.

11th July, 1934

The Air Ministry emphasises that it will help us honestly but one should not try making them believe things, because they are receiving *exact information anyway*. The next Air Attaché for Berlin, who is closely connected with Winterbotham, will be a good man as opposed to the present one, who is a rather simple-minded man. Corresponding to that the German Attaché will be shown round in England.*

Rosenberg's Report to Hitler of 12th May, 1934, is also relevant:

England's air-fleet, being smaller than the French one in numbers, presents some difficulty as regards parity. I have been working on this aspect for eighteen months, and I had already discussed these questions with a young British Officer in England in December 1931. This personal contact in London has turned out to be very productive. During the past eighteen months we have continually given London reports of the political situation. All British Staffs were kept informed about our political opinions which, unlike the British official news service, turned out to be true. This connection became more and more close; therefore Major Winterbotham decided to undertake a short *Urlaubsreise* to Berlin, during which I could introduce him to you.

The result of this conversation was that the British Secretary of State for Air was well pleased, and Baldwin, who was informed at once, justified the German desire for security in the British Parlia-

*Musterschmidt Verlag 1956

ment by explaining that the Germans in Berlin and the Ruhr might have the same fear of an air-attack as the English in London. After that Major Winterbotham sent a letter on an official sheet of note-paper from the British Air Ministry saying that he would send to Germany an English officer as a representative of a big British air-craft company. This officer came here with an official letter of intro-duction and has been in touch with the persons in question, and his single-minded work justifies hopes that, first of all the Air Ministry, and then the staffs of the other British service ministries, will bring increasing pressure on British foreign policy.

6

Reaction in London

I was totally unprepared for my reception back in London—a carpet, yes, but not a red one! Apparently the Foreign Secretary was not pleased either with my visit or with the information I had obtained. I could understand the first part since he himself had failed to get any change out of the Nazis and no doubt felt a little piqued. Hitler had told me that Anthony Eden and Sir John Simon had been over to see him sometime before I arrived in Berlin in 1934 and that he, Hitler, had left them in no doubt about his intention to build up a sizeable air force. He said he had not got on well with these English politicians; apparently the thing that annoyed him most about Anthony Eden was the impeccable crease in his trousers and his pointed shoes!

But the second part, why? If Eden and Simon knew of Hitler's plans in the air, then so did Baldwin. Why did he not want the detailed information I had been able to get? Both Vansittart, head of the Foreign Office, and Lord Londonderry, who was now Air Minister, were tickled to death; I gave them and Philip Sassoon, the Under Secretary of State for Air, a long personal account of my meetings. Here at last was something direct from the horse's mouth with which to encourage the Government to get on with the re-equipment of the Royal Air Force.

Alas, Lord Londonderry was not to remain in office; he eventually became the scapegoat for Baldwin's refusal to admit the necessity for re-equipment of the R.A.F. I was to get to know him better during World War Two through my dear friend Oliver Stanley, his son-in-law. Londonderry was too nice a person to fit in with the growing hurly-burly of the half-truth political life of the 'thirties, despite the traditional role of the family and the famous political receptions at Londonderry House. Both Lord Londonderry and Oliver Stanley were politicians of the old school, with a real sense of service and duty and, luckily for them, no urgent necessity to make quick money out of politics.

It was the reprimand by the Foreign Secretary that opened my eyes to the policy of *laissez faire* by the Government which was the reason why we found ourselves unready for a Second World War in Western Europe. Here, I think, we must digress for a while to try and unravel the rather complicated political situation in England which undoubtedly played into the Nazi's hands between 1933 and 1939.

Why should authentic information about German air rearmament in violation of the Versailles Treaty be apparently the last thing the Government wanted? True, that if that sort of information, and a great deal more besides, was accepted by the Government, then some action would be called for. This the Government seemed determined to avoid. Why did not the Labour section of the Coalition and, later, the Labour Opposition call for action to stop the Fascists? Was it because neither the Conservatives, nor Labour, were willing to risk the loss of votes by advocating a programme of even limited rearmament?

It is true that after the holocaust of World War One, which was supposed to end all wars, the people of Britain were not ready for another. We now know that Baldwin believed that any beating of the drum would result in a demand for an end to the Coalition and that whoever told the British Public the truth and suggested rearmament would lose the vital votes they needed to be returned to power. But if, for this reason, the Conservatives were anti-rearmament, Labour was downright pacifist, and it is possible that Baldwin and his colleagues also argued that if Labour came to power the state of affairs could be immeasurably worse. Nevertheless I think Baldwin was wrong.

Although I was so close to him in my work I never had personal contact with Baldwin, but from the time that I came back from Germany in 1934 I never trusted him. I have known him go into the House of Commons to answer a question from Sir Winston Churchill, on German Air Rearmament—in his pocket the latest figures which I had sent round to him at his urgent request that morning—only to get on his feet and reply that he had no information on the subject. His sell-out of Lord Londonderry as Air Minister was an unpleasant bit of political nonsense.

Much has been written about this outwardly benign but ineffectual Prime Minister. For a man who was political master of Britain for fifteen years it is in a way sad that his epitaph should be 'Failure', and his short paragraph in History the handling of the Abdication of Edward VIII. To me he will always be the boss who seemed deliberately to frustrate the efforts of those who tried to warn him and the nation of the impending disaster of World War II.

I personally believe that if Baldwin had stood up to the facts and unfolded the picture of the Hitler menace to the people of Britain, he could have fought and won the General Election of 1935 on the question of limited rearmament and that a harder attitude towards the Nazis would have been accepted. As it was, the first public indication that Baldwin was beginning to regret his studied refusal to acknowledge Nazi rearmament came in May of 1935. In a speech in the House of Commons Baldwin said, when referring to estimates of German air strength: 'I was completely wrong; we were completely misled on that subject.' The second half of his remarks was, of course, a downright lie and somebody had got to take the blame—but not Baldwin.

I do not know what went on in Cabinet but, to one on the fringes, it seemed to me that early in 1935 the pressure of Churchill and others in the House of Commons forced Baldwin to recognise publicly what he had hitherto deliberately suppressed. I think, too, that Lord Londonderry, the Secretary of State for Air, had refrained either by design or from mistaken loyalty to Baldwin's policy to pass on officially the information which the Air Ministry had, which included all that I had passed to them. For the same reason Air Ministry Intelligence were in no hurry to accept the information which I obtained in Germany. This my Chief would not stand for and told the Chief of Air Staff as much; he also notified the Prime Minister of his complaint.

There was some heart-searching in Air Intelligence where the young Flight Lieutenants did not stay long enough in their jobs; they were ever keen to get back to flying. A well-trained Intelligence officer must have continuity of work. He must, if possible, know the people he is up against and how they think and operate, and he must be able to develop a nose for false information.

I had been lucky in this respect and despite my daily contact with Air Ministry they did not always arrive at the same conclusions as soon as myself and had not presented their case to the Government as forcibly as I had. Whatever the real cause, with 'C's' complaint before him Baldwin took the opportunity he had been waiting for to let someone else carry the can. He ordered an enquiry into the whole subject of German air rearmament at Cabinet Committee level: at last the Government were taking action, or so I thought. On one side of the long table were three Cabinet Ministers with Cunliffe Lister, later Lord Swinton, in the chair. Opposite them, on the one half, were Lord Londonderry, Sir E. Ellington, Chief of Air Staff, 'Chris' Courtney, Deputy Chief of Air Staff, and members of the Air Intelligence Department. Further down were my Chief, myself and Desmond Morton, who later joined Churchill's staff at No. 10.

My Chief had warned me that I might lose my much coveted job if I failed to convince the Cabinet Ministers. Luckily, contact with top brass and politicians has never worried me. I also had the advantage of having seen the rearmament in progress in Germany under the personal aegis of Hitler. The meeting lasted three hours and I had to talk most of the time.

The result, I fancy, was a foregone conclusion, anyway. Honour was satisfied! Cunliffe Lister himself took over from Lord Londonderry as Air Minister and gave me all the support I wanted plus extra assistants which allowed me to devote more time to German affairs.

Despite the outcome Baldwin still took no action on rearmament, and, when Hitler marched into the Rhineland in 1936, neither we nor the French had any teeth to back up a No. Nor was it until November of 1936 that Baldwin finally admitted his mistake in not taking Germany's rearmament seriously. I quote from Hansard:

66

I put before the whole House my views with an appalling frankness. Supposing I had gone to the country and said that Germany was rearming and that we must rearm, does anyone think that our pacific democracy would have rallied to that cry at that moment? I cannot think of anything that would have made the loss of the election from my point of view more certain.

I believe he was profoundly wrong. The stakes were too high, the risks too great and our eventual loss too appalling to have passed up the chance to stop Hitler in 1936.

To give Baldwin his due, he did start making preparations for a few shadow factories. This could be done without raising much comment and it undoubtedly helped when, after Munich, Chamberlain too late gave the go-ahead to rearm, notably in the air; an almost breathless breathing space of twelve months which just managed to tip the scales in the Battle of Britain. From beginning to end it was a case of too little and too late.

7

Diversion

1935 was a busy year in London. Also I had to keep a close liaison with my opposite number in the French Deuxième Bureau which meant I went to Paris for about a week every three months. My French colleague and I would co-ordinate our information and discuss ways and means of checking on the material Bill de Ropp was now sending me.

In the early 'thirties the French had the Maginot Line of fortifications well under way and seemed completely satisfied about their security. Paris was relaxed and gay, the White Russian refugees were as proud of their new French nationality as they were, in 1944, of the exploits of the Red Army.

How comfortable were those flights from the old grass aero-drome at Croydon in the large Handley-Page 'Box-kites'; take-off about noon, a large leisurely lunch on a wide table in the spacious cabin; Le Bourget Aerodrome; the bus ride to the Place de l'Opera; the Champs Elysées in the spring, with the sweet-smelling chestnuts in full bloom; the fantastic night spot; Sheherazade with the tall Russian waiters—mostly ex-guards officers—dressed in their knee-length, high-collared scarlet tunics; the old rose velvet curtains, the dim lights, the persuasive wailing of the Persian fiddler; the franc at about two-fifty to the pound, and the *politesse française* still apparent.

I used to stay with my very good friends, Bill Dunderdale and his wife, who, at that time, had a flat just opposite the Guitrys' house, near the Champ de Mars. My hostess was a very lovely American girl; her husband, a colleague, had lived a long time in Russia and had acquired a famous chef from the refugee colony.

I must say, the Guitrys were far better entertainment off the

68

stage than on! At least once during each of my visits there was a splendid scene. Yvonne Printemps, superbly befurred and carrying only her jewel case, would come out of the house and whilst standing on the steps alternatively call for a taxi and hurl vituperation over her shoulder, where Sacha gave as good as he got, his famously melodious voice lost in an ever-rising crescendo of abuse. The lady returned the next day—I suspect it was her way of having a night off!

My arrival in Paris was the signal for an official French lunch. Service pay in France was never over-bountiful so a smack-up lunch on the expense account was very welcome. Seven or eight of my French colleagues would come along and we would foregather at a well-known restaurant on the point of the Isle de Cité, not far from Notre Dame. There, in a private room looking out over the pleasant gardens with their shady trees and to the accompaniment of the occasional chuff of a barge going up the river, we would eat food and drink wine fit for the gods. I suppose one can still obtain such meals if one is a millionaire.

We did not talk 'shop' and conversation inevitably turned to the best shows to see, the latest night-spots where the most beautiful girls were to be found. Did I know that the principal dancer at the Bar Nudiste who, quite obviously, had the most perfect figure in Paris, was married to a wealthy industrialist who collected her in his Rolls Royce every night after the show? Did I know the most beautiful of the nudes at the Bal Tabarin were English? How lucky we must be in England! As the lunch ended the younger members of the French party would begin looking at their watches and would be excused by their Colonel. Their bare wooden tables in their offices would see them no more that day, but the doors of the 'Houses of Pleasure, Officers for the use of' closed at three for the afternoon. The rest of us would sit on awhile.

I suppose the four of us, Bill Dunderdale, myself, and two of the top men of the Deuxième Bureau knew, as much as anyone, about German rearmament and the aims and plans of the Nazis. It was not a pretty picture. Towards the end of 1935 my colleagues were showing signs of depression which, of course, got worse as time went on and no one did anything positive to check Hitler. By

1937 they began to realise that an unfinished Maginot Line was not going to hold the new German might with its parachute troops, its dive bombers, massed tank units and the whole of Belgium open to them.

Defeatism, they said, was like an infectious disease and there were already those in France who thought a compromise with Germany at any cost preferable to another war. I was able to confirm this in Germany as early as 1936. Rosenberg had shown me a list in his office in Berlin of the French Collaborateurs and the amounts of cash they were being paid, but most of the names I did not know. Perhaps it was lucky for Laval, P. that he had a clean death by shooting at the hands of his fellow countrymen at the end of the war. Although I could not tell this to my French colleagues, I sensed that they knew all was not well in some of the top echelons. Our own doubts about France's will or ability to fight were to increase as time ran out; they were fully justified in their doubts about an unarmed Britain being of any use to them.

We all agreed that there was little more that we could do to prod the politicians into some sort of practical preparation for 'Der Tag Number Two'. We would stroll back to the offices of the French 'Second Bureau', a few bare wooden huts set up in a garden surrounded by a high wall close to Napoleon's Tomb. The stout green gate would be opened by the aged 'concierge', we would look left and right along the street to see that we were not being followed. One day our solemn procedure was interrupted by the arrival of a rather ancient open lorry, the blue bloused driver got out of his cab, took two mail bags from the lorry, threw them on the pavement and with a shout of *'voila pour les espions'* rattled off. We looked left and right once more and entered.

I was reminded of the true story of my chief the Admiral who, shortly after taking over as 'C', was arriving at the offices of the S.I.S. which were at the time in a quiet road in Kensington. The milk for the office 'cuppas' was also being delivered at this apparently quiet private house. 'C' casually asked the milkman who lived there and got the prompt reply 'The Secret Service', at least it gave 'C' a good excuse to move to more central quarters 'somewhere in Whitehall', though no doubt the local milkman is equally well informed.

Unlike the British, the French Secret Service used to employ a large number of women on espionage work. It suited the Latin temperament and they considered, probably rightly, that a good deal of useful information could be obtained in bed by a clever operator. There was, as they admitted, always the possibility of the girl getting too emotionally involved, when the game might work both ways but they insisted that on balance it paid off. 'Interesting' visitors to Paris were usually well looked after, but I never heard of the process being used to the lengths employed by the Communists of political blackmail and recruiting of agents under threat of exposure. The French were delicate in their handling of the matter, but the whole set-up operated by the 'security' as well as the 'information' departments was given a much wider authority than our very correct police procedure.

Whilst on duty in Paris I was told that I could get away with anything except murder—not that I had occasion to do so, but it gave one an extra sense of security when dealing with 'agents' in the capital.

Due to Bill Dunderdale's close relations with pre-war Russia, I mixed a great deal with the white Russian refugees in Paris. They were a strange, unpredictable, delightful, courageous collection of people. Those that had been able to smuggle out jewels had set themselves up in small shops or restaurants, many of the women-folk, delicate, black-eyed china dolls, ex-princesses, grand duch-esses and others formed little groups and sang Russian songs in the restaurants; borsch, blinis and vodka became the popular dishes and drink; the taxi-drivers, often ex-guards officers, settled down to their new job with a bit too much Cossack cavalry élan. A rather wizened ex-Air Force general who never stopped smok-ing Russian cigarettes, painstakingly and skilfully compiled for me a list of the new Russian Air Force Squadrons, and where they were stationed. Just how he got the hundreds of scraps of infor-mation from his contacts I do not propose to tell, but at a time when Moscow had put an iron security net around the country, his methods were very ingenious. Through hours of smoke-laden arguments I gradually learnt enough Russian to check and recheck these carefully guarded secrets of the Russian Air Force.

Despite the strange mixture of work and play in the Paris of the 'thirties there was a growing uneasiness that something was wrong somewhere at the top. The information given me by Rosenberg was again strongly confirmed by one of my most valuable sources in Germany who supplied vital information on the German Air Force. He never ceased to stress that on no account must the information be given to our allies otherwise his life would be in jeopardy.

On the outbreak of war the regular airlines stopped and I found myself once again in the open cockpit of an old R.A.F. single-engine aeroplane, with a pilot who had never before crossed the Channel: fortunately I knew the way to Paris by heart. When I told Lord Londonderry of these rather primitive arrangements he kindly lent me his twin-engined cabin aircraft complete with pilot, for which I was most grateful. I used it between London and Paris until the approach of the hot war put an end to it.

In the summer of 1935 I had to make an extended survey of Intelligence in the Near East. The Royal Air Force was, in the 1930's, responsible for the maintenance of security and good government in Iraq, Jordan and Palestine. Other countries were starting to smell oil and there were other indications of trouble-makers who were ever ready to undermine British influence in the area and add to our discomfiture.

Baghdad, Jerusalem and the Holy Land, Kurdistan—names that have always fascinated me, and at last I was to have the opportunity to see them, travelling in reasonable comfort by air. I say 'reasonable', for only once did I nearly have to 'jump' when the rather ancient R.A.F. aircraft in which I was travelling started shedding bits of hardware over the desert.

Perhaps one day the great inventors of new and power-mad ideologies will stop rocking the cradle of Western civilisation, and the Garden of Eden—that priceless stretch of desert between the mighty Tigris and Euphrates—will once again blossom into abundance.

Flying over ancient Mesopotamia is like looking at an endless crossword puzzle, so clear is the pattern of the irrigation canals which carried the life-giving water between the two rivers. Perhaps one of the greatest acts of destruction in world history was perpetrated here by Genghis Khan and his Mongols when they destroyed this food store of Arabia.

I flew up to Northern Iraq with the Ambassador and his wife and daughter, together with some of the embassy staff. We were to pay an official visit to one of the great sheiks of the wandering Bedouin who are virtually the only inhabitants of this inhospitable area. By modern standards we flew low over the desert and every so often we passed over a great mound of sand and earth. These were the remains of the great cities of the Medes and Persians, cities built one on top of the ruins of another for thousands of years.

The old Vickers Vimy transport plane rolled about the clear but 'bumpy' sky and I remember thinking how little the Colonial Secretary was going to enjoy the meal of greasy sheep we should soon be eating.

The size of the camp of black goathair tents spread around on the pale pink desert below showed the importance of the Sheik we were visiting: close by he had prepared an air strip.

We were greeted by a large, bushy bearded man, his flowing black cloak over spotless white robes. His Arab headdress and curved golden dagger denoting his sheikdom. Large brown eyes under heavy black eyebrows twinkled a welcome. The guard of honour consisted of a hundred strong young men ranging in age and height, the eldest about twenty-five and the youngest ten. All were dressed in spotless white and at a sign from their father they sang a very creditable verse of *God Save the King*.

Sheik Ajil was proud of his sons, though he explained that these were not all of them. He led us to his tent.

There were seven-foot-tall Nubian slaves as black as polished ebony who served the traditional bitter coffee. More slaves attended with silver bowls of rose water and little hand towels made in Lancashire. The Sheik had been advised that Lady Humpheries was not really keen on sheep's eyes for lunch so this traditional tit-bit for the principal guest was tactfully absent, but a whole roast sheep on its bathtubful of rice was good eating. My only complaint was the sand; it was hard to sit on and its inevitable intrusion into one's mouth as one tore the morsels of mutton asunder with one's now sandy fingers made for gritty eating.

The rich carpets spread over the floor of the conference tent, the colourful hangings on the camels, the giggles of the vast harem, seeing but unseen, were indications of the Sheik's wealth. No wonder Arabian nights hold a strange fascination for some Englishmen. Here, surely, was Abraham coming out of the north with his sons and his camels and his sheep and all his wives.

Perhaps one day scientists will find out to their amazement that the story of Noah's three sons was a simple reflection of a story from the beginning of time and that man did, in fact, evolve in three separate areas of the world; Central Africa, China's Gobi Desert, and the cradle of our own Western civilization—the land of the Kurds, in Northern Iraq. It would seem logical.

I was able to have a word with the Sheik's eldest son, and he confirmed my information that German railway engineers had been in the area. There was a German dream before World War One of a Berlin to Baghdad railway. The dream was presumably still alive with the added advantage of oil at the other end of it. It was just another straw in the wind blowing eastwards from Nazi Germany.

I met the old Sheik a year or so later when he came to London for the Coronation of King George VI. He was staying at Claridges and told me he found it very comfortable.

The Holy Land I think fascinates everyone. If only down the ages Christendom had refrained from building great churches over all the most Holy Places, and then squabbling amongst themselves as to who should occupy them. Alas, the pilgrim business has ever been lucrative whether to Mecca or Jerusalem, but there is one place in Jerusalem where I, at least, felt the compelling force of timeless belief.

I remember today the feeling I had there that if only I could have got Rosenberg to stand with me before the Rock in the cool serenity of the Temple at Jerusalem, he might surely pause in his pursuit of racial paganism and experience the feasibility of a power which would make a thousand-year Jew-persecuting Reich look something of a nonsense.

Diversion

Back to Cairo where the perpetually ineffective Pan-Arab conference was going on. It seems the Arab states have been talking about acting in unity for many years and no doubt will talk about it for many more, but Palestine looked like being a serious problem in the not far distant future. It was, but I was able to make the necessary arrangements to have the Israeli underground watched meantime.

8

Anglo-German Relations

I had had to rely on Bill de Ropp to keep me up to date on information during most of 1935 though I did manage to get over to the Nuremberg Rally in the autumn. We had had a bit of a flurry in the January of 1935 which I think is best explained by Rosenberg in his diary of that date:

> 21st January, 1935
>
> A few days ago Baron de Ropp came here again. Mysteriously; only for me and the Führer. His Majesty the King of England has expressed great astonishment to his political adviser, that England's information about the true situation in the *Saargebiet* has been very poor. The 'serious press', especially, had failed. This displeasure has caused much excitement. The adviser in question applied to the Air Ministry, which has always been in contact with me, and asked for a detailed instruction about the situation in Germany. Whereupon Major Winterbotham called de Ropp and asked him to come to London. De Ropp is going to meet the King's Adviser in a club in order to inform him about what is going on. Yesterday he left.*

There was considerable activity during the year on the rearmament front. The Nazis were taking the British Government's lack of action as funking the issue and seemed convinced that the more they thrust their vast rearmament programme down our throats the more embarrassed the Government would be, and the less likely to start interfering in Hitler's proposed squeezes on Austria and Czechoslovakia.

There must have been some criticism of Rosenberg's handling of Foreign Affairs in 1935. De Ropp reported that there seemed to be some changes taking place, and Ribbentrop was evidently trying

* Musterschmidt Verlag, 1956

to get the job for himself. Rosenberg's methods were certainly unorthodox and amateurish, but I doubt if Ribbentrop's were much better.

Rosenberg had suggested I should come to Germany for a good long stay in the summer of 1936 and see anything I wanted to. When I arrived I found a very different Rosenberg from the one I had met in London—more withdrawn, much fatter, sallow and a bit 'crumpled'. He was immersed in his ideology, preparing plans for the dissemination and control of his new religion, not only throughout Germany, but to include the rest of Continental Europe in the future, and was trying to put it across to the Finns and Danes, 'true Aryans' as he called them. He explained that he had handed over some of the conduct of Foreign Affairs in order to give himself more time to organise his Priesthood, but he had retained the job of keeping Hitler personally informed about foreign press comment and had trained a public relations staff to deal with foreign press correspondents in Berlin.

He was also flirting with the Free Ukrainians; this, I suspect, was more of an anti-Russian gambit than an exercise in Nordic propaganda.

One warm evening in our favourite little cafe bar on the Kurfurstendamm Rosenberg opened out about his pet plans. He told us he had actually started to build a great cultural centre, rather on the lines of an enlarged Vatican City in Southern Germany. It was to be the centre of the Nordic Cult throughout a 'unified' Aryan Europe (presumably by 'unified', he meant 'subjugated'). It was to have great colleges for the instruction of the Priesthood. I nearly asked him if it was to have a Stonehenge type circle in place of St. Peter's, but the poor chap was so carried away in his vision that I just kept quiet and listened.

Was Nietzsche's anthology to become the Nazi Bible? Perhaps this new Rosenberg, rather withdrawn, apparently lonely, more often seeking out Bill to talk in the little cafe, was preparing himself for his High Priesthood and beginning to have doubts about his ability to carry it out.

I had decided to spend as much time as I could in Germany during 1936 because I felt that not only might I not be welcome much longer but there were a number of points on which I needed to be perfectly clear in my mind. These were, firstly, to make a thorough check on all the reports I had received about air rearmament from other well placed sources in Germany. Secondly, to clarify the Nazi plans: when would they start a shooting war? Which was the priority—eastwards or westwards? What were the Nazi relations with the Army and what was the nature of the bargain Hitler had made with the Army: 'I have had to sell half my birthright to the Army.' This, I was sure, included some sort of agreement to neutralise Western Europe either by diplomacy or force, before embarking on Hitler's dream of the conquest of Communist Russia and the 'lands to the East'.

It was a fairly large programme and Bill was to tackle the political angle through Rosenberg. I wanted to get out and about and meet people—not only the boys and girls in the street who, incidentally, were growing excited about the future and had a very good idea of what was going to happen, but some of the more influential Nazis who would, I knew, talk to me if given the green light by Rosenberg. The year 1936 was going to matter to England. It was probably the last chance we should have of initiating a game of chess; as it was, we were not even capable of playing diplomatic draughts!

I think it would be appropriate here to give Rosenberg's report to Hitler on the question of Anglo-German relations. This was made in October 1935 and only became available in 1964. It was evidently his swan-song in the Foreign Relations arena.

A SHORT REPORT OF THE ACTIVITIES OF THE DEPARTMENT FOR FOREIGN AFFAIRS OF THE N.S.D.A.P.

October 1935

The task of the Department for Foreign Affairs of the N.S.D.A.P. could not from the beginning model itself on the Foreign Office, but was limited in a quite definite way. The following concrete problems were extracted from the whole complex of foreign policy.

The Anglo-German relationship, the north-east area, the south-east area (Danube area) in addition to the adjacent nations interested in it and Soviet Russia.

Recognising the fact that the entire foreign policy of today is most closely bound up with the question of foreign trade, a special organisation for reporting on this question also was set up. Thus the following sections were formed in the A.P.A.:

England, the North, the South-East Area, the Near East, Foreign Trade, the Press.

1. *England:* The attempts to find people in England who were eager to comprehend the German movement date back to 1929. Our English agent R. [de Ropp] in Berlin then made possible my first journey to London in 1931. There it was possible to make a number of contacts which worked out well for an Anglo-German understanding. In the forefront here was Squadron Leader W. [Winterbotham], a member of the Air General Staff, who was entirely convinced that Germany and England must move together toward off the Bolshevik danger. The outcome of the various discussions was the widening of the group amongst the Air General Staff, and the Royal Air Force Club became a centre for fostering Anglo-German understanding.

In the Spring of 1934 Squadron Leader Winterbotham came to Germany and was received by the Führer. The Führer's handling of this matter subsequently resulted in the strengthening of a policy which was already well disposed towards us, and since then permanent contact has never been broken. When there are anti-German activities in London, enquiries always come to us from the Air General Staff as to what reply could be made to favour the German standpoint. The German arguments have then been turned to good account wherever appropriate. Unlike certain English individuals who on the one occasion spoke out enthusiastically for Germany, only to declare the opposite after some months, this firm group in the Air General Staff, led principally by younger officers, showed itself to be firm and keenly aware of its goals in all uncertain situations. Not least of all Baldwin's great speech of the previous year, in which he conceded the right of Germany to air protection, originates from these influences.

The English magazine *The Aeroplane*, appearing under the sponsorship of the Air General Staff, has always strongly opposed Bolshevism and has declared again and again, when tempers were roused against Germany's alleged militarism, that today it would be entirely to be welcomed if Germany had a strong air force in order to ward off Asiatic barbarism. The English ministers who would not accept this viewpoint were most fiercely attacked. In a re-shuffle of the British Foreign Ministry it was not a candidate of the Francophile British Foreign Office who eventually became Foreign Minister, but the one-time Minister of Aviation Samuel Hoare who, still today, maintains his old personal connections with the Ministry of Aviation. At his request a Memorandum inspired by us on the intellectual foundations of National Socialism, has been passed to him, as he wishes to try to understand our Movement more fully.

During MacDonald's term of office direct touch was maintained through MacDonald's private secretary, Mr. Badlow, whom I had got to know in 1933 and with whom I had held detailed conversations. Since then he has been kept continuously informed by us and has more than once had heated discussions with MacDonald.

A positive result of the close liaison with the British Air General Staff was that contact between our Air Ministry and the British airmen was established. Yet before it was possible to make known our rearmament, Winterbotham, on the official paper of the English Air Ministry, informed me of a representative of the aero-engine factories which manufacture engines for the British Air Force. Later I received him here in Berlin also. However, as the German industry had already progressed so far, the almost official British furtherance of German air rearmament could not be taken full advantage of. At all events the leader of our English department (Kapitänleutnant A. D. Obermüller) had brought two representatives of the German Air Ministry to London and had undertaken several journeys to London himself. He was the first German to receive an invitation from the Air Vice Marshal to have a thorough look at British air power and equipment. The A.P.A., too, had put a car at the disposal of the Air Marshal when he was in Germany for a sight-seeing tour the previous year. A closer link between our English section and Henry Deterding and his circle has also been taken up. It was possible to straighten out the misunderstandings over the tax situation connected with Deterding's German property. This did prevent changes in the arrangements at Deterding's, or as the case may be, at the Shell works, the result of which would have been the loss to the German State of important commissions.

At the end of last year we were notified that the King of England had pronounced himself dissatisfied with the official press reports. The Duke of Kent's visit to Munich had only worsened the English King's opinion regarding official news reporting, and so one day we received the request from London to make it possible for our English agent to make a trip to London to explain about National Socialism down to the last detail to the Duke of Kent for the purpose of informing the King of England. After careful consultation with me, de Ropp travelled to London where he unobtrusively had a three-hour conversation with the Duke of Kent, who then reported it to the King of England. It may be accepted that this meeting contributed very greatly in strengthening the pressure for a reconstruction of the Cabinet and mainly towards beginning the movement in the direction of Germany.

On Party Day in 1934 a number of Englishmen were invited, some of whom at least were doing work which favourably concerned Germany. First and foremost was Captain MacCaw, the semi-official adviser of the English War Office and liaison officer for other Ministries. Formerly MacCaw had been an Adjutant of Lord Kitchener's, and, as we ascertained, has for his part worked in a commendable manner in official places for an Anglo-German understanding; and besides him, also, the adjutant of the Duke of Connaught (Uncle of the King of England), a man of sincerity and enthusiasm. Archibald Boyle was actively working towards the same end; he was the official appointed by the Air Ministry to deal with all foreign questions on its behalf. In addition to these most important contacts there are a great number of other acquaintance-ships with British politicians, officers and Members of Parliament.

It goes without saying that other people as well in the N.S.D.A.P. had important connections with England and took full advantage of these. All in all, however, I think I can say that, despite many difficulties and opposition, which I will not go into any further, the English section of the A.P.A. has done its utmost to help create the special conditions for an Anglo-German understanding.

9

Meeting the People

Bill had told Rosenberg that I wanted to get around a bit during the summer of 1936, so the latter had thoughtfully delegated a young member of his Press Relations staff to look after me, with instructions that I was to go and see whatever I liked. It was useful cover also, because any inquisitive outsider could be told I was being given the usual courtesy of a foreign press representative.

Karl Boëme—Charlie, as he liked to be called—had just become a professor, that title so beloved by the Germans, albeit he was only a Professor of the Press, a chair no doubt invented for members of Rosenberg's staff. He was a cheerful, good-looking young fellow of about twenty-seven or -eight, about five-foot-ten, fair, his shirt and breeches well cut. He liked to be smart; he was the joy of most of the barmaids on the Kurfurstendamm. He had a quiet, rather plump little wife who lived in Hamburg and who sometimes came to Berlin with her wire-haired fox terrier and terrible tweeds. I gathered that wives were not encouraged to appear in official Nazi circles—this was a man's world. There is a German expression which, literally translated, is 'a good Charles'—meaning 'a good fellow'—so I used to call Karl 'a proper Charlie'; he felt more than complimented.

The Nazis insisted that their members whose work entailed contact with foreigners should learn the appropriate language. Charlie was struggling with English and thanks to an extraordinary system by which they had to learn off by heart a hundred words of English a week, and then learn to string them together in the right order afterwards, he was progressing rapidly and gratefully used me to practise on.

Meeting the People

Rosenberg was due to visit Lübeck, that wonderful old Hansa city on the Baltic, for a few days. He suggested that Bill and I should go, too, and Charlie was to ensure that I saw and did anything I wanted. It was mid-summer and hot in Berlin and we were only too glad of a chance to go to the sea; also a chance to see that historic city. The drive up was rather dull, the country flat, and the roads at that time were not as good as those further south.

As usual, when a high Party official was due, forests of crimson banners festooned the city, ruining the lovely old buildings. I think these banners must have been transported from one place to another as required; I simply cannot believe that each town had such a large collection. There was not the same warmth or enthusiasm as further south—the Baltic folk have always been an independent lot and they were a bit cautious in their enthusiasm for the Nazis. Nevertheless, there was a small crowd waiting outside the principal hotel to see the arrival of Rosenberg; he therefore advised the canter technique into the hotel.

The following day was Midsummer's Day and Rosenberg proudly announced that he would take us to see the new Nazi version of the Festival of the Solstice. No doubt this was one of his main reasons for coming but he had been a little nervous about telling us in case we had found some excuse not to come. He was keen to show us some of 'his own work' in the ideological field. Maybe he found the Baltic folk more interested in the Pagan Rites than the South Germans; worship of the sun-god probably fulfilled the primitive needs of our forefathers when it came to bad harvests and low fertility.

I thought we might be in for the sort of ceremony performed by the present-day Druids at Stonehenge or perhaps some singing like the choir on the top of Magdalen Tower at Oxford, colourful reminders of our own pagan origins. We climbed to the top of the old Lübeck Castle. In the centre of the gravelled ramparts was the circular top of the ancient keep and now, as we approached, we saw that within the circle of the keep roof was another circle of identical Hitler Youth, shoulder to shoulder exactly the same height and shape, fair hair, blue eyes, totally Aryan in their pale khaki shirts and shorts. Their leader in the centre was accompanied

83

by two identical acolytes. Rosenberg and his party took their seats and the battlements echoed not with the clank of armour or the whistle of arrows but with the centuries older pagan litanies and chants. At mid-day there was a shadowless silence as the sun hung for a moment directly overhead, and then a paean of praise for a Nordic Sun God. I wondered if there was to be a sacrifice?

The whole performance had been in deadly earnest. Here was no lighthearted compliment to tradition. Here the youth of Germany were being indoctrinated with a new creed, the creed of their own racial superiority, of the glory of the state, reflected in the Sun, a creed which could only breed arrogance and hatred, war and conquest.

It was like an unpublished chapter from the *Experiment in Time*. Despite the sunshine I did not like it at all, but of one thing I was sure, the Youth of Germany would at this time have set up any false gods their Führer had told them to.

We are told that, even up to the time of William Rufus, human sacrifice existed in England, though by then it was confined to the head of the state. When the plight of the people got too desperate from bad harvests the flight of the arrow in the woods was no accident. Was this Nordic nonsense going to revive the human sacrifice? As Rosenberg watched the performance with enthusiastic approval, he answered my question: No human or live sacrifice was made in the Nazi version of the Festival.

Recently he had had considerable trouble with an ex-general up in Schleswig whose fervour had induced him to seize and sacrifice one of his farming neighbour's best cart-horses and then to lead a barbaric dance round the corpse, stark naked. This was apparently going too far and, much as the Party needed distinguished military adherents, the general had had to be stopped in the face of local disapproval: all this with a dead-pan expression. How little time was to pass before the human sacrifices beyond the comprehension of even barbaric pagans were being made in the gas-chambers.

That evening, in our hotel, I tackled Rosenberg on the whole subject of his new or, perhaps, rehashed ideology. I was already aware from his remarks when we were in the Luther country that he held the Christian religion in some contempt. I knew, too, that Precept Number Two of the Rules of Dictatorship is that all existing religions must be supplanted by the virtual worship of the State. The Nazis had identified this with the Nordic race and it was a logical step to return to the paganism of their Aryan ancestors.

Looking back, I suppose I was pretty critical of Rosenberg's new religion; maybe I went a bit too far, but I tried hard to point out to him that if he had any regard for history—and history has an uncanny way of cropping up again—then his plan to eradicate all the old beliefs and customs which had been used down the ages, albeit too often abused by ambitious priests, would surely alienate a large part of the older population who might otherwise go along with the Party.

The successful dictatorship must have, as we know, both an internal and an external enemy. In the U.S.S.R. it is still the 'spies and saboteurs', coupled with the fight against the 'imperialist reactionaries'. In Germany, given the new Nordic Cult, the internal enemy was *ready-made*—the Jews; the external enemy, the Communists, the potential destroyers of the Third Reich.

It is probable that history, in the long run, will remember Hitler and his henchmen for their greatest evil—the murder of countless millions of Jews. This wholesale slaughter did not start until long after I stopped going to Germany. Persecution was, at that time, confined to the wrecking of Jewish property, like the jeweller's shop in the Kurfurstendamm which I saw sacked by a carful of howling young Nazis; or the extortion and confiscation of money. Lucky were those poor families who got away alive during that period.

I had argued the Jewish question with Rosenberg at his home in Berlin and had left him in no doubt that the Nazi policy of Jewish persecution was probably one of the main reasons why the United Kingdom had given Hitler neither help nor encouragement. He told me, and I think he was telling the truth, that he was trying to establish some sort of refuge for the Jews in Brazil. It never came off, but I find it hard to believe that the gas-chambers were contemplated by the Nazis in the early days. I believe they hoped

85

that the persecution they were then adopting would force the Jewish families to leave Germany. Figures have been given showing that about half of them did get away, but for countless thousands—where could these poor unfortunates go?

There is a story of a meeting at Evian when the Nazis offered to sell the Jews to the Western democracies at a hundred pounds apiece but that the money was not forthcoming. I have never heard it confirmed. Maybe if the conquest of Communist Russia had gone according to plan, there would have been some sort of resettlement of Jews in that country. I think when their plans began to go wrong their latent bestiality emerged. Unlimited personal power, unrestricted by any ballot box, will ever turn a human into a tyrant and a failing dictator into a maniac. The killers amongst them went berserk. I do not believe that either Rosenberg or Hess were real killers. Rosenberg gave the killers their cue with his Nordic nonsense, so he cannot escape the collective moral responsibility of the whole bunch.

I had got a bit hot under the collar.

Perhaps to cool me off a bit, Rosenberg suggested a day or two by the sea at Travemunde by way of relaxation. Travemunde, by the Baltic Sea, is an attractive spot in high summer. Now it appeared to be a place of relaxation for more senior Nazi officials. There were a number of them there with their wives or girl friends. The large modern hotel was 'well appointed'; whether it was part of the 'Strength through Joy Organisation' I never found out, but it was gay with the girls in their summer frocks; there was dancing in the open air and cool drinks.

Several Nazis and their womenfolk had been asked by Rosenberg to join our party. Charlie was becoming a little restless. No selection of seductive blondes was drawn across my path; however, I did notice a very striking girl, obviously of Southern Slav origin, who seemed to be attached to one of the officials, and asked who she was. This was his cue. She was brought over and introduced to me. I looked into a pair of the most mischievous eyes I have known. We danced. Her escort was found some very urgent business in Hamburg that very afternoon.

Josephine was a Yugoslav from Zagreb, well educated and speaking several languages. Her exquisite little figure, her dark sloe eyes beneath her raven hair, her gaiety and philosophy of live, love and laugh had inevitably led her to the stage. As a dancer in Berlin she had soon become the toast of those Nazi officials who were junior enough to escape the 'image' of celibacy imposed on the top lads.

I think that Josephine and her friends taught me more about the feelings, the reactions to propaganda, and the exhilaration of the young German at finding a purpose in life than anyone else during that summer of 1936. It was a small piece of the pattern of the desperate effort of the Nazis to wean Britain from any obligation to fight a war.

It was at Lübeck that I made my first contact with the new German Navy. Two brand new destroyers had just been completed and the 'Top Brass' and politicians were to see them put through their paces. Rosenberg was to represent Hitler, who did not like the sea. Other Nazi officials included the head of the armament programme but, to the evident annoyance of both sailors and Nazis, von Fritsch and a number of his General Staff Officers decided to come, too. This was interesting. The Army was establishing its authority over the Navy, maybe as a result of Hitler's deal with them; the Army was not going to let the Navy get close to the Nazis as the Air Force had done under Goering. The situation, I sensed, was a bit tense. Even Rosenberg showed contempt for a young army officer, grandson of the great Bismarck, who slithered all over the decks in his incongruous jack-boots, ordering matelots out of his way.

Out at sea the little ships raced about at great speed, laying smoke screens and firing dummy torpedoes; a thoroughly good exercise and show off by the young navy. Rosenberg, anxious to escape from the Army on the way back to port, took Bill and me down to the Junior Officers' wardroom. The young men with whom we had drinks were a different cut from the army types; sons and grandsons of German naval officers of the old regime, nicely mannered boys ready to talk—perhaps excitedly—of their hopes for the new German Navy, of the cruisers and battleships being built, and keen to hear an airman's opinion of the 'ship versus aircraft' controversy exercising the minds of sailors everywhere. Later that evening, at the get-together in Lübeck, I had a delightful talk with an elderly and very courtly admiral who had been an A.D.C. to the Kaiser for a number of years.

Apparently the Kaiser had had a passion for strawberries and he used to start a yearly pilgrimage in Corfu in early spring, gradually working his way northward across Europe as the strawberries ripened, ending up in East Prussia or Norway in the autumn. The admiral got sick and tired of strawberries, but the Kaiser never.

The old admiral was quite interesting, too, about the design of the new battleship *Bismarck* which was then building. He was expanding on its gunnery control and its unsinkability due to the vast number of watertight compartments when Charlie, who was with me at the time, grew panicky and fetched Rosenberg. I told Rosenberg all about our interesting discussions; he seemed pleased, but the admiral, alas, closed up.

One of the main reasons why the Air Staff could not, and the Government would not, bring themselves to believe the figures of German rearmament in the air, was the vast programme of training that this sort of expansion would entail. The Air Staff did not envisage the possibility of training so many thousands of pilots, mechanics, signallers and all the specialised anciliary personnel required for a large Air Force in the time available. Pilot training was one of the items I had been very closely quizzed about at the 'showdown' at the Cabinet Committee meeting I have already described, and I lost no small opportunity to see and hear personally all that I could on this subject.

I had managed to find out that, with the thoroughness and innate love of precise documentation of the Germans, Goering had set out the whole organisation, training equipment and operational roles, of each German air unit down to squadron level in a set of volumes which I should dearly have liked to get my hands on. It must surely have been a very closely guarded encyclopedia. Nevertheless, I did receive a limited number of photostatic copies of various pages of these volumes, which gave an unanswerable guide to the complete set-up. One such page had listed the names and locations of the large number of Flying Training Schools.

This at least was a good basis to start on. Now I had to try to see some for myself.

I had noted considerable activity at the Navy's Flying Training School at Wannemunde, so I made an excuse to take Josephine back to Travemunde for a week's holiday shortly after. The Kurhaus Hotel was comfortable; the sun and the sea and Josephine's gay chatter and companionship made the time pass only too quickly.

Just across the canal which ran in from the sea was the new flying training school. I watched and listened as we lay on the sandy beach; it was not difficult to estimate the daily number of hours flown.

It was during this short exotic holiday that I first really began to meet and talk with the ordinary young boys and girls of seventeen and eighteen. Josephine sensed my interest in their talk and their views, her gaiety at once attracted them and the fact that I knew their Führer gave me an automatic entry to their company.

I don't know whether this was Rosenberg's intention when he took me to Travemunde, but it certainly worked out the way I wanted, and for the whole of my stay in Germany during that hot summer of 1936, I used Josephine shamelessly, but nevertheless willingly, to contact and talk with the 'boy and girl next door'.

I don't think anyone who just passed on official opinions or propaganda handouts either through diplomatic channels or the press, fully realised the extent to which the fever of excitement at the coming fulfilment of their dreams of a great German Empire, in which each one of them would have a goal and a purpose in life, permeated the hearts and minds of the youth of Germany in the middle 'thirties.

Laying aside all the horror, madness and beastiality of the 'party line', there was something so genuine in the enthusiasm of these young Germans, one sensed an irresistible force, the force of the youth of a whole nation fired with an ideal yet, alas, woefully ignorant of the means which would be used to attain it. How often I heard the argument that the whole conception of overwhelming military forces was to ensure that there would be little bloodshed, and that in the event Germany would be hailed as the Saviour of Europe.

The idea that they might again have to fight the English had not occurred to many of them. They had no doubt accepted the 'logic' of their Führer that, in the strange event of England being ungrateful enough for Germany's war against Communism to enter the conflict against her, the matter would be dealt with quickly and almost painlessly.

I give these impressions just as I received them. This was the time for the young people. They would make their own exciting world! Goebbels was certainly doing his stuff. It was a new experience to watch the harnessing of mass endeavour; if only it could have been for real progress. I followed up the question of training when I got back to Berlin where I was now an Honorary member of the brand new German Air Force Club. I have described a little later in this book how the Club came into being, and how I was looked upon as having provided the inspiration for its birth. Anyway, I had the official green light and the young members were quite prepared to talk to me about their training or 'crash courses'. My views were once again confirmed. I now wanted to get a look at a number of the new training aerodromes, to clinch the matter. A large number of them were situated in the ungetatable area to the East of Berlin. My chance was to come soon.

Back in Berlin a few days later I was asked to a splendid outing, organised by the new Reich Stage Artists' Association. Josephine had arranged for me to go along and on a misty dawn at one of the quays on a Berlin canal we boarded a little paddle-boat, and with hot coffee and flamboyant greetings from old and young companions of the stage we set off down the canal, out onto one of the big lakes north of the city and away to a sunny little island, complete with cafe and restaurant. They were a cheerful crowd and the beer flowed!

The doyen of this offshoot of the 'Strength through Joy' movement, a sort of collective recreational organisation, was a matinee idol of the 'twenties, with eye-glass, white blazer, white flannels with a broad black stripe and heels just a little too high. His lady companion, in flowing chiffon, wore a large shady hat a bit out of place on the paddle-boat, but at least it betrayed no secrets.

One young man whom Josephine introduced to me had just

joined Goebbel's Propaganda Ministry. 'Well,' he told me, 'it was either that or the army, now. Lots of extra bodies are being recruited by Goebbels.' We got on very well and as I left him he remarked to another companion when he thought I was out of earshot: 'He seems a good sort of Charlie—it's a pity we've got to fight them.' He had evidently read his new brief.

10

Erich Koch

Erich Koch was a veritable cock-sparrow, born and brought up in the Ruhr in Western Germany, a railway worker by trade and a passionate Socialist. He saw no future in the trade union movement under the Nazis, so wisely joined them to achieve his ambitions another way. He was a born organiser and all his stocky five-foot-six oozed energy. He was always smiling, at least when I saw him, which was fairly often.

He had got the job of Gauleiter of East Prussia which was virtually cut off from the rest of Germany by the Polish Corridor. Here he felt he could carry out his plans with the least interference from Berlin. I liked this enthusiastic man as soon as I met him; he had none of the arrogance of the Prussian or the jumped-up Nazi about him, and he was terribly anxious that I should go and see what he was up to in East Prussia. And so on a summer's day in 1936, in a special flight JU 52, Charlie, Bill and I set off from Tempelhof for Konigsberg.

I had asked Charlie to let me see as much of the country east of Berlin as possible. I don't think anyone who doesn't look at maps has any real idea how far east Berlin really is, and how surrounded it is by forests and lakes which seem to spread forever eastwards into Russia. As one flies over this country the water in the little lakes glistens in the sunlight like so many mirrors, nestling in deep green velvet forests which stretch away to the horizon on every side. There are a few areas of good land and it was here, to the east, that so many of the new military aerodromes were being built. I told Charlie to ask the pilot to see how many we could count and, bless them, they found and flew over most of those within reasonable range of our direct route.

These aerodromes were all much the same pattern, designed for one or two squadrons but now packed with training aircraft, and the skies around us were buzzing with trainers. This was certainly an opportunity I would not have missed. It was the visual proof of information from my ground sources, which the Air Staff had found it difficult to believe. To those who had spent their lives in the Air Force, not even familiarity with the training programme of the R.F.C. in World War One could compare with the present effort in Germany; it was prodigious.

We had to land at Danzig for customs. It was not difficult to imagine the irritation of the Germans at this restriction, one of the less sensible provisions of the Versailles Treaty. Nevertheless, the famous Danzig *Goldwasser*, a sort of Cointreau with specks of gold leaf floating around in it was welcome, and the blonde Polish barmaid was duly noted down in Charlie's little book. On leaving Danzig, we flew on along the Baltic coast and up the long canal leading from the sea at Pilau to Konigsberg, some miles inland.

Erich Koch himself was at the aerodrome to welcome us with his broad smile and a noticeable lack of *Heil Hitlers*. We joined the waiting cars at an ordinary walk. The hotel was good, clean and comfortable, and the food was excellent. The tensions so evident in Berlin seemed entirely lacking, the only real one being anti-Russian.

Konigsberg was the only permitted air contact-point with the U.S.S.R. at that time and I saw some forlorn-looking bearded Russian officials being given the treatment on reaching German soil. Koch, like Hitler, really disliked the Communists, perhaps his main point of contact with his Party.

Erich Koch was a friend of Rosenberg, although I got the impression he used his friendship more to get what he wanted for his beloved 'Province' than by way of any admiration for Rosenberg's theories, as he called them. I had met Koch in Berlin and from my short conversation with him I had gathered that his passion was the planning and carrying out of a full-scale resettlement scheme largely for the overcrowded families of the Ruhr. Frankly, I don't think he cared two hoots about Nazi-ism except that it could, and did, give him the power to carry out his social reforms.

The morning after our arrival we went round to the Town Hall to see Koch's Planning Department. This was in the charge of a very pleasant young Jew—Koch had no time for anti-Semitism.

Much of the country in East Prussia is taken up with forests and lakes, but there is still plenty of good land which, if properly cultivated, could produce plenty of food. In the Masurian Lake District, near which was fought the famous Battle of Tannenberg, the scenery is magnificent. I have little doubt as to what has now happened to that rather attractively designed octagonal Shrine of Remembrance to Hindenburg's victory over the Russians. The Victory of Tannenberg was a very precious memory to the Germans and, in a way, offset their defeat in the west in World War One. They had set up a lecture hall with a large relief map hanging like a cinema screen, on which the progress of the battle was indicated with coloured lights to the accompaniment of a lecture by one of Hindenburg's ex-staff officers. I saw a party of young officers of the new Army come out of the hall quite starry eyed.

Erich Koch came to East Prussia in order to put into practice his dreams of resettlement and as he took me to one after another of his new towns or 'settlements'—as he called them—he explained in detail all the plans he had for the future of this little land. He bubbled over with enthusiasm.

The first thing he had found out was that practically the whole of the agricultural land in the country was in the hands of the old Prussian families—von 'This' and von 'That'. But these gentlemen had not bothered to make their vast estates pay; in consequence they were all pretty heavily mortgaged to the state. There had been some sort of fiddle by which the landlords did not even pay any interest. It was, therefore, easy for Koch to foreclose these mortgages and take over the land. He did, however, leave the barons enough land around their houses to run a home farm and to continue to call themselves 'von' and 'what have you'; at least, this is what he told me and I certainly saw some examples of it. It was a wise move, for the barons did not mind very much, as long as they had somewhere to live; many, I think, were relieved at not having to worry about their lands and their mortgages.

One family had certainly got things straight. Koch took us to spend the night at a plain, square-built baronial hall not far from

Elbing. We arrived a bit late in the evening and I had not known quite what to expect. Koch told me that the Baron was away but that the Baroness would look after us. I envisaged the legendary length of high-necked, tight-busted ankle-length black alpaca between buttoned boots and a screwed-back bun. The stout doors were opened by an aged retainer in knee-breeches and as we were ushered into the lofty, softly lit, heavily-panelled hall, a very beautiful woman in a white gown which had not stopped on its way from Paris greeted us. At first sight I thought it must be Marlene Dietrich herself, so exactly alike were they; later, she told me she was Polish, which explained both her elegance and her vivacity.

I do not know whether the Baron was away permanently, or just making some cash in the capital, but the house turned out to be a sort of 'welcome home' for a select few of the higher Nazis when they came to East Prussia. Goering used it as a hunting-lodge when he came up after moose and deer, Hitler himself had been to stay, and I feel sure my very attractive hostess gave them a good time. It would have been interesting to hear more from her. We dined and wined from the best, little Erich Koch doing more than justice to his second helpings.

There was a son of the house, a boy of about fourteen, swarthy, totally unlike the Baroness; I think he must have been the son of a previous wife. He had evidently been trained by his father; once, when the old retainer had not jumped to his command, he sent him flying through the baize door with a kick and a curse. The Junkers still thought they were in charge in some places.

I slept in the special bed which had been built to hold Goering; at least there was plenty of room to move about.

When Koch had chosen a site for one of his settlements, instead of building the house in the middle, he put the factories and light industries at the centre, on the railway or river. Most of the light industries he brought out from his native Ruhr, together with the people who already knew how to operate them. The living houses, shopping centres, sports grounds, swimming-pools, etc. were then located outside the factory area with plenty of roads leading in. The houses, in this way, could be planned on a garden suburb principle with all their amusements close at hand.

Outside the housing belt again there was a ring of small-holdings for those small farmers who preferred to produce vegetables and perishable produce. These holdings had only to deliver into the housing belt and need never penetrate the industrial centre at all. Outside these small-holdings again were the larger farms growing grain and live-stock. Such a set-up could never have been attempted unless whole areas of land had been available from the start; the idea seemed good and Erich Koch was immensely proud of what he was doing.

There was no false showmanship, either, when we visited a number of houses without any warning; the new tenants were generally delighted to see Koch. He admitted he made the initial mistake of putting the bathrooms downstairs. The old habits of keeping the coals in the bath die hard, and so upstairs went the baths, where it was too much trouble to carry the coal, anyway!

It was summer-time and the sight of so many kids from the Black Ruhr enjoying the open-air swimming-pools was refreshing.

Elbing is a typical small old-fashioned East Prussian town, built on three sides of a large gravel square perhaps two to three hundred yards across, all the houses whitewashed and with red-tiled roofs. At the far end stood the stalwart building of the Town Hall and, one side or the other, a few three-storey buildings, one of which was the local hotel. It was here we came to have lunch on our way to see the historic Hanseatic castle of Marienburg.

As usual our party, Erich Koch, Bill, Charlie and myself, and one of Koch's boys from the Planning Department, arrived without notice. However, the hotel readily agreed to put on lunch. The landlord, anxious to honour the Gauleiter, promptly told the mayor; and the mayor and corporation insisted on coming, too— all three of them! This, in turn, meant getting an extra waiter. The one they found was out of practice and in his nervousness spilt the soup all over my suit. There was panic! I think the mayor suggested shooting at dawn, the landlord just a year in jail; however, my assurance that no harm was done, together with a tip to the waiter, seemed to restore the situation.

Marienburg was originally built in the late thirteenth century, about 1280. It was enlarged in the fourteenth century and was the seat of the Leader of the Teutonic Knights. In the great hall is a series of richly painted murals showing the history of this Hansa outpost which was half trading-post, half castle, much as the old trading-posts of the East India Company used to be before the British Government took over India.

Our guide was, I think, an ex-Prussian officer of World War One, still very stiff and correct, complete with eye-glass and duelling scars. The first mural showed the Prussian peasant in the days when Marienburg was first built. To my surprise they were wearing only bearskins and carried wooden clubs; even our rural population of the thirteenth century was becoming slightly civilised and I pointed this out to our guide. He nearly exploded; his stiff collar managed to contain the reddened neck with valour! At last, unable to insult me in front of Erich Koch, he turned on his heel very precisely and strode off. I had no idea the Prussians were so touchy. Koch burst out laughing, which did not improve matters.

However, we found an old caretaker who showed us over the rest of the castle. One could imagine those early traders watching from the battlements, looking down the river for the approach of the stout Hamburg ships. Marienburg must have been a very isolated place in those days, almost like Moscow itself.

Hess was due to visit Konigsberg the next day. I woke up to find the town a forest of red banners and very excited. There was to be a sports display by the youth organisations and an opera in the evening.

Hess was staying at our hotel, the only good one in Konigsberg. He was his usual quiet self and, no doubt due to the calmer atmosphere of Konigsberg, a little more relaxed than when I first met him in his spartan office in Berlin—just round the passage and down the stairs from Hitler's own fabulous room. After the usual displays by Hitler Youth and rows of buxom young women I was walking away from the sports stadium a few paces behind Hess, down a broad corridor of grass between a living, impenetrable wall of six-foot tall, black-uniformed, white-gloved, steel-helmeted giants standing shoulder to shoulder. I marvelled at the security technique which the Nazis had worked out and I remember thinking how different was this man strolling rather shyly alone towards his waiting car from the ordinary run of strutting, saluting Nazis one saw back in Berlin.

We went to the opera that night and I sat next to Hess. The local company had chosen *Coriolanus*, principally because every few minutes someone gave someone else a Hitler or Roman salute, which seemed to amuse Hess but did not impress him. He was much more concerned with the low standard of the singing and the music. He talked of music, which he evidently enjoyed, though I gathered he did not share Hitler's passion for Wagner.

There were a number of naval officers up from the submarine base at Pilau for the occasion and after the opera it was suggested I should go down the next day and see the place. I was promised a rousing evening in the mess. This was a tricky one. I knew where I was when Rosenberg suggested any of these trips but I thought it better to keep my nose clean where submarines were concerned.

I did, however, avail myself the next day of the opportunity to see an amber mine in East Prussia. There are, I believe, only a few in the world. It was closely guarded; amber in large lumps like potatoes must, I thought, be a pretty useful commodity. But it was only when we returned to the cleaning and processing plant after visiting the great open-cast mine that the manager got worried and, taking Charlie aside, he asked if it was all right for foreigners to see what was now a war factory. Charlie gave him the okay and laughed with us over the idea of our seeing anything we shouldn't.

In fact, the amber was being melted down and purified to make some particular kind of fine resin for covering electrical wiring. I did not go into the matter too far in order not to appear too interested or to embarrass the man in charge. It seemed such waste of a lovely material which was, I suggested, valuable for necklaces and beads, especially in the Moslem countries, but I was assured that the market for necklaces had been cornered by the British and that, anyway, the resin was unique for certain classes of insulation at extreme altitudes. The answer to that one only came in 1944.

Apparently the reason for the amber's presence was that in the dark ages, when this whole area together with the Baltic Sea and Scandinavia was covered in great pine forests, some giant storm or meteorite had felled a wide swarth of trees right from East

Prussia to Sweden. The pines, cut down in full vigour, had oozed great lumps of resin which, in due course, had been buried and turned into amber. That part of the amber bed which now lay under the Baltic was continually washed by the sea, which accounted for the bits of amber we used to pick up on the beach at Felixstowe, on the East Suffolk coast, when we were kids. It was uncanny to see what looked like ordinary flies and mosquitoes encased in great lumps of transparent gold and to realise that they were perhaps millions of years old. There did not seem to have been very much evolution in those species since then; maybe, unlike the human, they had already reached their full state of usefulness as scavengers before Man evolved.

There was one other place in East Prussia I wanted to see before, perhaps, it was gone for good and that was the great Stud Farm at Tracheneu. Before World War One this used to supply nearly all the horses for the German cavalry regiments; goodness knows how many mares were kept in those days. When I was there in 1936 this lovely stretch of rolling grassland was only partly occupied. The vast paddocks with their white wood railings were dotted with clumps of oak and pine for shade. In the centre of the farm were the stud buildings erected round an enormous quadrangle. The whole scale of the place was prodigious.

Even now, a number of paddocks were full of the most lovely horses. Four colours were bred here—chestnut, grey, bay and black—and I suppose there were about fifty mares of each colour running with their foals of the year. Other paddocks held the yearlings, and still more the two-year-olds. I gathered that there was some system of putting them out on farms as two-year-olds until they were fit to go to the few remaining cavalry units, or perhaps to private ownership now the cavalry was all but finished. Any one of the horses I saw would have made a good hunter. The stallions were nearly all imported, either from the United Kingdom or from Ireland. To anyone with a love of horses it was a wonderful sight.

I was sorry to leave East Prussia. Here was a little state, untroubled up to now by racialism or Hitler salutes, being transformed from its feudal harshness into a well-planned social experiment, Erich Koch its benevolent dictator, a man who put people before things. And now, as we flew back above the long straight canal leading to the coast and over the sand-dunes which divide a large inland lake from the Baltic sea, both Erich Koch, who was flying back to Berlin with us, and I looked down rather sadly troubled at what was in store for this land. We both knew. He asked me to come back again.

11

The Pace Quickens

I had spent a great deal of time in Germany in 1936 and it was not until September 1937 that I once more flew to Berlin. I believe that this was a critical year in Germany. Somehow one felt that in official circles one was being treated a little more carefully. By contrast, the American Press and visitors were being given the full V.I.P. treatment. Young Hearst, of the Hearst Press, already very Anglophobe, was the subject of a great deal of attention by Rosenberg's Foreign Press Department. The Military seemed a little more sure of themselves; the German Air Force, with Goering's new Air Ministry now complete, were so busy getting their units organised that they had no time for visitors. However, having successfully negotiated the unstoppable open-fronted lifts of this new Air Ministry, I was courteously received by the officer in charge of foreign liaison. The year before it would have been the signal for a drink with some of the old-timers.

In 1934 I had invited a group of young German Air Force officers who were officially called members of a civil flying club over to a civil flying rally at Heston Aerodrome, and had put them up at the Royal Air Force Club. The visit gave me a useful 'contact' with the new Air Force in Berlin. As a result, a replica of an English Service Club had been set up in Berlin and, here, in 1936, one had been well entertained, with talk all about the new types of German aircraft. But late in 1937 the atmosphere was much more formal. I felt an alert sounding and in consequence, whether in Berlin or Nuremberg, I took good care not to talk out of turn.

Charlie Boëme, too, was becoming rather inquisitive. I was in his professorial office one morning when, quite casually, he asked me: 'What slogans are you going to use for the next war?' Evidently this was a leading question from Goebbels' Ministry passed on to me as received. How useless to tell him that we did not work out these things in advance and that, anyway, His Majesty's Government did not recognise or, rather, were busy ignoring the possibility of war. I was quite sure I was not believed when I denied any knowledge of such plans, and no doubt Goebbels' worst fears were realised when their own Beethoven gave us that incomparable V-sign.

There were only a few days to go before the Nuremberg Rally which, this year I gathered, was going to be 'colossal', partly to impress the Italians who would be attending for the first time and partly as a counterblast to the Army who were getting a bit uppish now that their turn was coming. Charlie was still very friendly, and as Bill was working hard on Rosenberg Charlie and I had time to look around.

I had had Charlie Boëme over to England early in the year; I felt it would do him no harm to see London and a little country life in Gloucestershire. He watched a typical meet of the Cotswold hounds and was curiously impressed with our pink coats and top hats; to him this was very old world stuff! In London, we were taken out to dine at the Savoy by the Wenningers. He had now been promoted to colonel and made little pretence of not being a full-blooded air attaché. He hadn't brought enough money so I lent him some. While Charlie was trying to bewitch the cloak-room girl with his English, Mrs Wenninger tore her husband into little strips. They had been very tense and anxious to show up well in front of young Charlie. Hitler's hierarchy was potent.

How lucky were the Berliners to have large lakes all around them; just a fifteen-minute tube ride out of town and you are on the sandy shore of the Wannsee, with swimming, sailing and sun-bathing. All the young boys and girls seemed slim, blonde and brown. Maybe they had not too much butter to eat, but physical fitness was evidently regarded as one of the outward signs of the Master Race; they were certainly picturesque and full of life.

I was surprised to see several Jewish families on the beach. The Nazis appeared to have stopped their open persecution of these unfortunate people. I wanted to tell them to pack up and get out before it was too late but I had to be careful. As it was, Charlie and I and Josephine came under close scrutiny—the reason?— two obvious Aryans with a young woman, her lithe body tanned a deep brown, and her jet black hair contrasting sharply with that of her two blond Aryan escorts. It was not until they saw her tip-tilted nose that the hard glances relaxed. It was a new experience to be at the possible receiving end of racial discrimination.

Yes, Berlin was gay that summer for the boys and girls. Kranzler's Restaurant on the Kurfurstendamm was packed out, and the pavements in the evenings were crowded. True, it was difficult to tell whether you were being accosted by a boy or a girl, but that was not unusual in Berlin. The Kakadu Bar did great business, though now it was more or less given over to foreigners, and Charlie preferred the little bars with more intimate barmaids. There was a spirit of: 'Let us make merry for tomorrow . . .'

Rosenberg was very preoccupied but one evening at his house— just Bill, Rosenberg and me—stands out in my memory. He had asked us to come round at six o'clock as he wanted to have a long chat. He lived alone in a big house with a couple to look after him. Curiously enough he had a television set there in 1937. Whether it was on a closed circuit with the Opera House, or maybe something of an experimental nature (the Telefunken Broadcasting House was close by) I don't know, but we watched a very good ballet on a fairly large screen; the picture was excellent.

Throughout a long drawn out meal starting soon after we arrived—champagne and sweets later followed by fish and meat courses embellished with estimable hock, on to fruit and sweets again, then to a tall bottle of sticky, sweet, green liqueur— Rosenberg was quietly giving me a warning of what was to come. I sensed this was the last time that I should see him intimately. He had learned a great deal of diplomacy since we had first met but this evening—perhaps it was the liqueur—he let his hair down and became more expansive than I had ever known him.

He told me that 'now that the Rome-Berlin Axis had come into being the Germans and Italians were very close indeed and, in fact, were exchanging all sorts of information'. What he meant was that they now knew my real occupation. I had good reason to believe that I and others were on the Italian list of those who wouldn't be missed. There was an unfortunate tie-up between the French and Czechoslovak Intelligence in Paris and quite recently the Czechs had also tied up with the Italians. It was undoubtedly through this connection that I and my colleague in Paris had been 'leaked' to the Italians. My suspicions had been aroused when I went to Italy in August, 1936; I was well shadowed all the time I was there and until the Paris Express from Rome again crossed the border.

Nevertheless, I think Rosenberg was genuinely sorry to feel this so-called friendship would now have to cease. Despite the fact that I had proved a complete disappointment to him in my supposed role of persuading influential people in England to see things the Nazi way, he again reminded me of Hitler's conversation about their policy of a triumvirate for the world. I think they still hoped to bring this off despite England's present refusal to play. He reminded me, too, that Hitler believed, and in fact all those in close contact with the Russians believed, that unless Communism was crushed, the world would degenerate into chaos; that the Third Reich could do it and were prepared to go it alone if Britain would, as he put it, 'for once keep her nose out of other people's business.' He said this with one of his rare smiles, but had he not accurately summed up the occupational disease of some of our more loquacious socialist do-gooders.

He referred to an incident the previous year when he had shown me proof of the bribery of certain French citizens by the Nazis, and suggested once more that militarily and morally France was not an ally to lean on.

He assured me that the German Army and Air Force was becoming the most powerful weapon ever known in Europe, and, finally, his own little bit about the Aryan races being the only ones who could rid the world of corruption. What more did England want?

Despite the intimate manner in which he told his story, and the generous draughts of wines and liqueurs, he must have prepared himself carefully for this conversation. He summed up with some skill all that the Nazis had been trying to put across to the British Government for the past four years. Little wonder

the Nazis were puzzled by the apparent lack of reaction; there
was none.

By the time we finally said goodnight he was really sloshed; he
could hardly stand up on the pavement, and was morose and sad.
I was sorry to say goodbye to him like this; we had, after all, had
some interesting, and even exciting, times together. He had always
given me the full V.I.P. treatment when I was in Germany, and
with his help I had seen more of the German country and its
people than most foreigners, and all for free. He had afforded me
the opportunity to see and check for myself much of what our
secret agents in Germany were reporting, and to sift the wheat
from the vast amount of chaff which was pouring in from refugees
hoping to turn in a spot of cash. But mainly I felt I had been able,
through close contact with the top boys and the great help of Bill
de Ropp, to obtain a fairly accurate impression of what was
shortly going to hit us, and how.

I have tried in the preceding chapters to give an idea of how the
pieces of the jigsaw gradually fell into place, and I shall try to sum
them up shortly in much the same way as I presented them to
His Majesty's Government at the time.

Next morning, when I did not expect to see Rosenberg again, he
rang up to say that would we care to go south with him on our
way to Nuremberg. He wanted me to see something of Bavaria
before the Nuremberg show. I felt a bit sorry for this misguided
and somehow unhappy man who evidently felt that he had been
a little under the weather the night before. Perhaps he didn't
want me to carry away a last impression of him in his cups; maybe
he thought I might still be useful in some way. Now that things
were getting more serious I wanted to get everything out of
Rosenberg that I possibly could and naturally took advantage of
his offer.

His chauffeur, as usual, drove superbly. He had driven me a
great deal on our various excursions around Germany and on Bill's
suggestion I had bought him a small gold cigarette case as a
present. Schmidt was embarrassed and almost sentimental; he
probably guessed that I should not be seeing him again.

We went straight to Munich and did the three hundred and

seventy odd miles in time for a four o'clock pint of that wonderful dark brown Munich beer, swallowed ice cold at a little café in the shade of the great cathedral. First impressions are often best. It was hot, the beer went down smoothly, and not all the Brown Houses or Streets of the Nazi Martyrs could dispel the charm of the place.

The new motorways, the plans of which had once preceded me at my first meeting with Hitler, were now operational and we drove down into the Bavarian hills to a favourite holiday haunt of the Nazi hierarchy, the Tegelsee. Much to the disgust of the locals, the large and prosperous *gauleiters* used to wear the traditional *lederhosen*, or leather shorts, and Tyrolean hats, which is much like a Londoner donning the kilt and the bonnet to go to Scotland for his holiday. The pants did not suit most of their figures, either! Nevertheless, the country was lovely. We met several of Rosenberg's friends taking a refresher before the Nuremberg show.

We went back to Nuremberg by way of the mediaeval walled city of Regensburg, now deservedly a tourist attraction. All was bustle in the town of Nuremberg when we got there. A new hotel had been built to accommodate the principal guests and Nazis of importance for the Rally. Companies of 'Brown Shirts' from various parts of the Reich were arriving and marching through the streets to those entirely German short staccato marching songs. They would be lining the routes for their Führer during the next week. The whole city was, as usual, a mass of crimson banners. Every now and again a well-known leader would go by in a large black car and the crowds would give him a *heil*. Especially popular was the town's own leader, Streicher, who was the main Jew-baiter. He was a really nasty-looking type who took his ill-gotten popularity with evident joy. Despite the grimness behind all the bustle, what with the multitude of odd-shaped brown-shirted Teutons, the crimson-bannered streets and the spotlights, I felt we were getting right back to the comic opera atmosphere once again!

Streicher had fitted up an anti-Jewish exhibition. It had large photographic murals of a well-known Jewish film actress, in all stages of nudity and love-making around the walls. This 'decadence exhibit', as it was called, made the place almost impossible to get into or out of, so thick, on the ground, were the gooping young Aryan males. Apparently some foreigner had taken away one of the crudely illustrated propaganda booklets and when I got back to my hotel room I found a tall blonde, dressed in a smart blue uniform, quietly going through my luggage. She got up from her knees quite unembarrassed, gave me a sweet smile, and explained it was just routine control. Needless to say, it was not I who had taken the booklet. We parted good friends but obviously everyone was being carefully watched. Bill confirmed this and we took good care not to talk privately in our rooms which were no doubt controlled by microphones in this new building.

This year, for the first time, the whole place was full of Italian officers in gaudy white uniforms, tassels, etc. I doubt they would have lounged about so happily if they had understood what the Nazis were really calling them. However, Charlie, Bill and I found a small bar free from Italians, with only Himmler and a few of his pals propping it up. The barmaid was after Charlie's heart, too. There was an entrance to this small bar from the street; it was carefully guarded, and one of its double doors was shut with a bolt into the floor. All at once there was a clatter of side-arms and a curse and there, stuck in the single doorway, was Goering. The quickness of Charlie saved the day. He slid up the bolt of the second door and the bulk flowed into the bar, beaming.

One trick I always enjoyed, and that was the way the 'Leaders' were both divested of, and re-equipped with, their Sam Browne belts complete with daggers and revolver's, their hats and, lastly, their gloves and canes. One of the Leaders had only to enter a hotel or other room from out of doors when two arms would come around his waist from behind, undo his belt-buckle and shoulder-strap and deftly slide the whole thing off from the back. Another pair of hands would remove his hat and then take his gloves and stick. I once timed Himmler being re-dressed in this way: three seconds flat!

Himmler looked at you with his beady eyes through his thick-lensed rimless glasses, yet never seemed to see you; perhaps he was only locating your jugular vein for future use. His handclasp was cold, his black uniform befitting the poisonous beetle that he was. He had no social graces whatsoever.

Rosenberg had arranged a luncheon for some of his more honoured guests at Nuremberg. The table was long and narrow and, as it happened, I was just opposite Himmler. After the usual heel-clicking introduction and the cold handshake, he spoke not one word to me across the two feet of tablecloth during lunch. It was more than probable he now had a dossier about me in his pocket. It was like eating opposite a cobra!

Each day of the Nuremberg Rally there was a show put on in the Sports Stadium, both for the benefit of foreign visitors and for internal propaganda. The Nazis, as usual, performed *en masse*; I think one of the most significant demonstrations I saw was the parade of the *Arbeitsdienst*. This organisation was really a form of pre-military training, designed to give young men of between fifteen and eighteen a grounding in discipline and to keep them fighting fit and out of mischief. It followed on after the boys got too old for the Hitler Youth Movement. The lads of the *Arbeitsdienst* were in camps all over Germany and they undertook all sorts of improvement work—roads, reservoirs, drainage, forestry operations and what-have-you.

I had spent the day at one of those camps on an earlier visit and I have seldom seen a more exuberant bunch of young men. The answer was, of course: they had a 'cause' and were kept busy in its service. If only the 'cause' had been different.

I asked the commandant, who was nearer twenty than thirty, how he kept the obvious high spirits of these lads under control. 'One teaspoonful of bicarbonate of soda per head per day,' he said, 'and sex doesn't even start to rear its perverted head.' The *Arbeitsdienst* drilled with polished spades instead of rifles and it was quite a spectacle to see some hundred thousand of them flashing the highly-polished symbols of their work in faultless unison.

Hitler was watching this particular parade and with my usual 'Royal Box' seat I was but a few feet away from him. Charlie, who was sitting on one side of me, seemed that afternoon to be completely hypnotised by his Führer; his eyes never left the Little Man's face, and from time to time he would interrupt my attention from the weaving and flashing of the spades with a dig in my ribs and words such as: 'Look! The Führer smiles. Look! The Führer laughs. Look! The Führer waves his hands.'

I could see it myself. I had never encountered this sort of absolute hero-worship before. I thought then that if Charlie could so lose himself in the worship of this little man, no wonder the youth of the nation were ready to go through fire for him. I certainly could never see the English young going overboard for a political leader.

It is indeed a sombre warning against the emergence of any future be-swastika'd Messiah. Maybe the Prussian element has had a setback; maybe the Second World War taught the Germans something of the folly of attempted conquests; but younger generations are apt to forget the horrors they never really knew. Maybe if television had been in full operation in Germany in 1937, and the closely guarded Party ceremony which I was allowed to witness at Nuremberg could have been shown to the public, some of the glamour of their leaders would have been a bit tarnished.

This Party get-together was, in fact, the annual Festival of Remembrance for those Nazis who were killed in the early days of the Movement. It was held in the new Party Hall at Nuremberg; under one of the two pillars of the doorway had been buried a copy of *Mein Kampf* and under the other a copy of Rosenberg's book *The Myth of the Twentieth Century*—probably the best place for both these works. The hall was not very large and only selected Party Members and their womenfolk were given tickets. I think Bill and I were the only outsiders and, as Rosenberg's guests, had again been given seats in the front row. On a raised platform a few feet away from us and facing the audience sat the Leaders.

The ceremony started soon after we had taken our seats. On the stroke of the drum, everybody stood up; and up the aisle from the rear began the slow procession of the banners. The square storm-troopers in black uniforms, their square heads engulfed in square black steel helmets, each carrying a square black and silver banner of his district surmounted by the inevitable vulture, slowly filed past the Leaders to take up stand behind them. At last the final banner was in place, making a great black and silver curtain behind the line of chairs on which the Leaders sat.

I had never before seen all the top Nazis together and now here they were facing me, all sitting in a row on hard wooden chairs not a dozen feet away. It just could not be true; they did not really look like that. It was almost like being in Madame Tussaud's! What was so odd about them? Of course, they had not their hats on. What an enormous difference the German military-type hat with its high front made to the wearer. But here, amongst their closest followers, they were just fellow-Nazis; no pale blue uniforms and rows of medals for Goering; now they all wore plain brown shirts.

I suppose any line of middle-aged men all dressed alike, but so different in size, shape and face, would look funny. I managed to keep my face serious by reminding myself that these men would be responsible for goodness knows what suffering, and I remember wondering what would happen if some fanatic or would-be martyr could liquidate them as they sat there together—Hitler, Hess, Rosenberg, Goebbels, Himmler, Goering, Heydrich, Ribbentrop, von Schirach, the lot.

Only Hitler and Hess seemed really at ease. The former had learnt a strange measure of self-control since his earlier carpet-biting days. Now, as he came to the lectern to read the names of his dead comrades, he looked not four but fourteen years older than when I first met him; the pockets beneath his protruding blue eyes were deeper, the face sallower; but the voice was strong and, as with other men whom I have seen fulfil their destinies in a short space of time, one sensed an authority which had not seemed quite so assured in earlier years. He had been the undisputed leader of this new Party since its inception; now all who saw him knew it.

Sitting on Hitler's right, Hess, the ever-faithful shadow, self-effacing, quiet-mannered, a dreamer, and yet, as he proved later, a man of decisive action if the need arose. I cannot think that Hess, a little fanatical perhaps where the welfare of his leader and his country was concerned, was basically evil, like some of his comrades. His solo flight to England at enormous personal risk fitted his character and was his last desperate act to save his country from inevitable defeat from a war on two fronts. As he sat, quietly smiling, next to his leader, his arms folded and the well-shod leg thrust out in typical pose, he, too, was relaxed.

But there was always a slightly wild look in his eyes below those bushy black eyebrows.

Alfred Rosenberg, who sat next to him, found his seat a bit hard. He often adopted a forward leaning position which he now held, one elbow on the knee and chin in hand. He had so amply repaid me for his first visit to London; when in Germany I had always been given a place of honour amongst his own friends. His hair was beginning to thin on top, his face had lost any youthful look it ever had and was now lined, pasty and flaccid. He seemed to be looking inwards these days, perhaps not quite liking what he saw. He was much more concerned with the long-term picture and now the moment of truth was coming nearer, with the stakes not quite so neatly arranged as he and his Party had hoped. Perhaps he was calling on his pagan gods; he looked as if he was sitting in the dock with his fellow-criminals—maybe he had a premonition.

Goebbels I never knew. He looked like an evil gnome, yet they say he was passionately fond of his family; a master of his art, but his task grew too big even for him. He sat now, his bright dark eyes darting from face to face; perhaps he was trying to get some inspiration for a new slogan; maybe, after Charlie's failure, he was trying to read my own mind. At least he stuck to his leader to the end. Unless you are insane, it takes guts to sacrifice your whole family and die with them.

Goering: now when you are as vast as Hermann and have short legs into the bargain, it is not easy to sit for long on a normal-sized, hard wooden chair and keep smiling. Despite the carefully arranged gaps on either side of him, he bulged against his comrades and seemed to look to them to keep him upright. He fidgeted, scowled, smiled mechanically from time to time. He also got overheated and had to mop his great slab of a face; signs of too good living were pretty obvious; I would say that Goering, unlike Rosenberg, lived for today and possibly tomorrow, and as we know, he did it in style. He was one of the great swash-bucklers of all time—Nero must have been one of his heroes—and yet here, in his vast brown shirt, buttoned up to the neck and down to the wrists, a plain black tie below the sweating face, he looked more pathetic than ridiculous. Power had sapped his better judgement, he seemed nearer to the point of demoralisation than his comrades.

Himmler never moved; he sat solidly rock-like, his arms folded. Only his eyes were never still, I suppose from force of habit, in much the same way as we fighter-pilots in the First World War kept looking all around to see who was getting on our tail. I never saw Himmler smile; always the cold, sinister, rather flat, pasty face with a bluish chin; the man who built up the black-uniformed storm-troops as his personal army, his own instrument of evil, as well as a warning to the generals. I believe this was the man above all others who uncovered and nurtured the beast which was never far beneath the surface of that band of sub-human monsters who gravitated to his banner. Like the rogue animals of the jungle, the more blood they shed the more they wanted.

Heydrich who, if it was possible, outshone his master, Himmler, in brutality. He was destined to be known as Heydrich the Hangman.

Ribbentrop always looked a bit out of place amongst these men, the sort of man you would never look at twice in ordinary circumstances, a man who showed himself during his time as ambassador in London as quite inadequate to fulfil any job requiring any intellect, tact or diplomacy, which after all was what he was supposed to have.

This was the last time I saw any of these men except Rosenberg. Somehow the comic opera had turned to sinister melodrama. The presence of such a concentrated dose of Nazis left me thoroughly depressed and I was thankful to get out into the sunshine and fresh air. Bill and I thought a drink was indicated.

That evening Rosenberg was waiting in the hall of the hotel as we came down for a drink before dinner. One of his aides in-formed me that he wished to say an official goodbye. Rosenberg was now a *Reichleiter*, next in rank below Hitler. As he stood erect, flanked by his staff and his bodyguard, wearing a new well-cut uniform with his badges of rank at the collar, he was at the peak of his career, one of the most powerful men in the New Reich.

He bade me a rather solemn farewell. I detected a little sadness in his voice. I felt sorry. Utterly misguided he may have been, but he was honest in his own belief in what he was doing. Alas! the revival of the Teutonic tribal gods let loose passions which we hoped had been buried by Western civilization—how deeply?

I left Nuremberg for Paris by the night train. Charlie came to see me off. Poor Charlie, everything was going his way; no wonder he became a little overwhelmed by his success. Here he was, in his thirties, already a professor, his wife safely tucked away in Hamburg with her white-haired terrier, all the girls in Berlin crazy for him. The wine was good, even the German champagne drinkable.

It was the German champagne that was eventually his undoing. I heard, sometime after the war started in 1939, that Charlie was as usual at one of the cocktail parties for the neutrals in Berlin. Russia was now a German ally but I think that neither the Germans, nor the Russians, were under any misapprehension as to who was fooling who. Charlie had too much to drink at the party and spilt the beans to a neutral of the plans for the great assault on Russia.

The word got back to Rosenberg of this unforgiveable indiscretion, so Charlie was packed off as a private to the army under orders to be sent to the Russian front when the time came, to put matters right. I expect he was in one of the penal battalions; anyway, I only hope for his sake that he did not last long—life in those battalions on the Russian Front must have been absolute hell. Bill, who was in Switzerland during the war, heard all this from contacts over the border.

It is difficult to describe the atmosphere that I left behind in Germany at the end of 1937, but the accumulation of impressions topped up with a subtle froth of suppressed excitement made me feel that it was time to try to piece together all the little and big events and conversations I had witnessed and taken part in during the past few years.

If I could add to these all the information I had gathered from other sources, I ought to be able to arrive at a fairly accurate conclusion as to the objectives, methods and timing of this Nazi cum Army set-up which we should assuredly have to fight once more in the not far distant future if the present policy of our own government continued. Perhaps parts of the analysis which I did at that time could be called intelligent guessing, but it was founded on well-formed impressions.

Impressions are important. All too often those responsible for assessing information are inclined to insist on chapter and verse in black and white; but intelligent impressions formed over some years of close association with the people concerned—the turn of a phrase, the odd remark at the end of a good evening, the odd silence when something should have been said—all these are, in my opinion, of more real value than collated items of sometimes doubtful origin.

The Deputy Chief of the Air Staff, who was one of my bosses, invariably asked me for my 'impressions' on the various aspects of German air rearmament. It was time for a re-cap.

12

Hitler Tames the Generals

Up to now in this book I have tried to give the impressions which the Nazis tried very hard to put across to me. If they seem a little light-hearted it is because that was the way they were presented, but the iron fist in the velvet glove was always visible through the holes, and the serious ideas were repeated to me from time to time Altogether, if I had not had the opportunity to study the information coming out of Germany which showed the other side of the coin, I might have been fooled by the apparent sincerity and friendliness of the top Nazis.

I had, however, taken the trouble to do my homework even before I came to Nazi Germany for the first time, and I was aware of the early history of Hitler. I had, as a prisoner-of-war in far-off Schweiduitz, witnessed the return to that Silesian town of the local regiment of the 'unbeaten' German Army in the winter of 1918. We as prisoners after the armistice were allowed our freedom until we could be sent back to England, and I was told by a friendly German officer how mad the men were because they felt they had been let down by the politicians and the Brass Hats in Berlin.

It was this resentment which first fired Hitler's imagination to once more make Germany great. Whilst he was still in the army in Munich, he joined one of the many small political parties which sprang up during the post-war chaos. Communists came and went, violence was rife, and in the midst of it the Nazi Party was born.

It was in 1920 when Hitler finally left the army, where his commanding officer had been the ill-fated Röhm, that he finally took control of the National Socialist German Workers' Party— the Nazis. Röhm gave Hitler his backing and from that time forward Hitler was the Leader. Anyone who suggests that he was only the puppet of his colleagues is right up the wrong tree.

From the start the Nazi Party was anti-communist, albeit there were a number of very left-wing members, and it was from this element that Hitler first recruited a band of thugs called the S.A. or Brown-Shirts, whose job it was to beat up all opponents to the Party and get it a name for toughness and action.

Three years after he had taken over the Party, Hitler felt he had enough support with the aid of the S.A., now about three thousand strong, to seize power in Munich. He also counted on the support of no less a person than General Ludendorff, one time Chief of Staff to Hindenburg. The coup was a fiasco and it was in the march of the Nazis through the streets of Munich that they lost sixteen of their members, shot down by the police. Rosenberg had been in the march and had narrowly missed being shot himself, or so he told me. These First Sixteen headed the Roll of Honour I had seen Hitler read out at the intimate Party meeting I had attended in Nuremberg.

Ludendorff's support had proved ineffectual and the Army certainly did not like this upstart. Hitler was sent to prison, but not before his name had become known outside the borders of Germany.

This was, I think, the first seed of mistrust between Hitler and the Army, a seed which was to emerge from time to time throughout the next twenty years.

We did not hear much of the Nazi Party again until about 1928 when, having decided to get power the constitutional way, Hitler barnstormed up and down the country. He was a dynamic speaker, there is no doubt. I don't pretend to understand the psychology of crowd mesmerism but undoubtedly he had a gift which appealed to the Teutonic mentality. By 1928 the Party got nearly a million votes, with twelve seats in the *Reichstag*. Rosenberg was one of these, and he told me of the turbulent time he had.

Then came the economic chaos which followed the American slump, a chaos which gave the Nazis their chance. In the 1930 elections the Nazi Party got six and a half million votes and one hundred and seventy-two Deputies in the *Reichstag*. The Communists took seventy-seven seats.

The Weimar Republic was tottering, and now Hitler wanted money badly. It is to the discredit of the German industry and banks that they now thought Hitler the better bet and let him have it. In return Hitler disowned the left-wing members of his own party.

1932 was another year of political chaos in Germany. In England we got so used to reading in our papers about another general election in Germany, but in July of that year the Nazis won two hundred and thirty seats in the *Reichstag* with fourteen million votes. Hitler now saw the Chancellorship within his grasp. Too late the Army now realised that their role as the power behind the throne was in danger.

Before World War One the German Army, or rather the great General Staff, were more than just soldiers; they were an integral part of the social and political life of the country. To be an army officer was the ambition of most young Germans; all doors were open to them, their officer corps was conducted on very strict social rules of marriage and behaviour; they were the élite of the land, and the generals had as much say in the affairs of the country as the civil government. The defeat of the Army in World War One was a bitter blow to their old prestige; nevertheless the old spirit remained, and gradually, in the late 1920's, the generals began to prepare for a revival of their old power. There was a secret arrangement with the Bolsheviks under which German officers and N.C.O.s were trained in Russia.

It was not surprising, therefore, that with Field Marshal Hindenburg as their President, the Army said 'no' to Hitler, but the Nazis now outvoted the *Reichstag* and dissolved it and by 1933 the Army could no longer hold out against Hitler. He became Chancellor in January. The new ruler of Germany had got there constitutionally and very largely through his own amazing efforts. The *Reichstag* was burned down in February of 1933.

It did not take Hitler long to outlaw the Communists, murder their leaders, and so, with complete power in his hands, he embarked on his totalitarian regime. Now his only rival was the Army and, in 1934, the generals became a bit restless; they did not like the way things were going. If anyone was going to rule Germany as a Dictatorship, then it should be the Army. In addition, too many Communists were now transferring to the winning side and joining the S.A. Brown-Shirts, and the man who now championed the left wing Nazis was none other than Röhm, head of the S.A. Röhm was getting a bit too powerful for Hitler's liking.

It was one of those hot summer days on 1st July, 1934, when the public gathered on the little aerodrome at Hendon to see the Display of Aerobatics by the Royal Air Force fighters of those days. The 'oo's' and 'aah's' of the crowd rose and fell with the loops and rolls and dives of the aircraft, and the Top Brass of the Air Staff held extremely tightly to their wicker chairs in the V.I.P. enclosure.

I had a guest, a member of Rosenberg's staff, A. D. Obermueller, who had been brought over by de Ropp. He had, I think, been duly impressed with the skill and brilliance of the flying. As we were leaving the airfield I saw a newspaper boy; the banner headlines gave the news of the shooting of Röhm. I showed it to Obermueller. I thought he was going to faint.

He held onto my arm tightly and said: 'Thank God we got him before they got us.'

I noticed he didn't thank Thor or Hitler. He left that night for Berlin. I learned later that he became head of an intelligence unit at Hamburg which worked against England. I had news of his inefficiency from time to time.

The 'night of the long knives' is now well known; there was much murder, but the S.A. ceased to exist as a threat to Hitler and at the same time appeased the Army to some extent. But Hitler was cunning enough to set up a really formidable force in its place and by 1935 the S.S. Storm-troopers were a formidable reminder to the generals not to try any funny business. Nevertheless, if Hitler's plans of conquest were to have any meaning he needed the Army and a powerful one at that, and so, even in 1934 when I first met him, he had evidently come to some arrangement with the generals to live and let live. His remarks to me about 'selling half his birthright to the Army' must have referred to some agreement, the first outcome of which was no doubt the elimination of the S.A. as a force.

But I believe the main bargain was that the Army should

remain as an independent political stabiliser alongside the Nazi
Party, as in the pre-1914 days; that they should be given a free
hand to run their own business of re-arming the Reich, and that,
in return, they would see the necessary finance was forthcoming.
I also think that there was some sort of bargain about Hitler's
war plans, such as the Army's right to refuse to go to war in the
West and the East at the same time and, in fact, the neutrali-
sation of Britain before they would fight in the West at all. I
don't think any documents on this subject have ever been discovered but somehow the above suggestions fit the facts and
behaviour of both parties during the next four years, as I saw them.

By 1935, after Hindenburg's death, Hitler was President as well
as Chancellor and the arrangement with the Army was working
reasonably well. The Communists and the Jews were being
subjected to the basic Nazi philosophy of murder, elimination and
terror. The outwardly respectable smiles of the Leaders, for a while
at least, appeared to cover the thuggery on which the Party had
been nurtured.

But despite outward appearances, it was evident to me that the
Army-Party relationship was an uneasy one; it did not fit in with
Hitler's conception of absolute power. Was this the thinly papered
crack that we should have found and exploited? We might have
had some success before 1934, but after that the Nazis were too
well prepared. Some approach was made to Fritsch who was
known to be opposed to Hitler's wars and thought Germany could
get all she wanted by strong military blackmail.

From odd remarks dropped by Rosenberg in 1936, the Nazis
were not satisfied with the independence of the Army. Hitler had
already won over a few generals to his way of thinking—
Reichenau, for one; and it was Reichenau who had put through
the order for all officers and men of the Army to take a personal
oath to Hitler. And now that the Army was expanding many of
the new recruits were already confirmed Nazis. Hitler was
gradually edging out the Army as a political power.

As I have said, 1937 seemed to show an intangible change in
Germany. The gaiety and good times for the young, so evident in
1935 and 1936, were tinged with a little more grimness, the attitude of the Nazi and Air Force people I came across had become

more formal. Things were shaping up. Hitler had already given us his views on a unified Europe under German control and a conquest of Russia, both to get living space as he called it, and also to finally destroy communism. Unless he could come to some arrangement with Britain, it was obvious he would have to do the Western job first, and it seemed very obvious to me in 1937 that he would not have much difficulty in that direction.

The arguments were once more repeated to me: if only England would fall in with their plans, for a Tripartite World Government, then there was some prospect the Americans would also. After all, France had neither the will nor the armour to meet the New Germany. Britain was still primarily an Infantry Army, without any prospect of stemming German Armoured Divisions. Surely the British would be neutral and let Germany make some compromise in the West so that the full German might could be turned against the West's worst enemies, the Bolsheviks? This was the theme which had been put across for the previous five years with a mixture of persuasion and show of force—the occupation of the Rhineland and a subtle effort to intimidate us by letting us know a good deal about their army and air force build-up. I was but one of the people subjected to both methods.

I remember one party of eminent British Aeronautical Engineers being given the red carpet treatment on a tour of German aircraft and engine factories. They were shown the latest production lines of fighter aircraft and one of them told me on return that the whole set-up was terrifying. It was meant to be. The Nazis had every reason to believe it was overwhelming and *still* there was neither action nor reaction from the Government in London, which left one with a desperate sense of inevitability.

And thus it was, in this hardening atmosphere of late 1937, that I had had a last plea from Rosenberg at our dinner in Berlin, and an official farewell at Nuremberg which might have delighted protocol-minded Whitehall, but plainly said: 'You have been warned.'

Early in 1938 the generals, fearing a premature war, made a last attempt to exercise their ancient authority in order to postpone military operations and curb Hitler's impatience. But it was too late, and Blomberg and Fritsch were dismissed. Hitler took over as Minister of War, with his faithful 'yes-man', Keitel, as head of the armed forces. Once again the Army was subdued and this time it took its place as a servant of the State and not as one of its rulers.

We had missed any chance there might have been of widening the gap between Hitler and the Generals. From now on we should have to deal with Hitler.

13

Flying Visit

1938 looked like being a pretty grim year. We were completely unprepared for war—we usually are—and the government continued to dodge the issue though most people had begun to realise we should have to fight Germany again in the near future. People's minds were taken off the German question a good deal by the Abdication of the King; nevertheless, the pace was hotting up in Germany. The Army had taken over security which was being buttoned up and information was harder to get.

I asked Bill if he thought it was still safe for us to take up Erich Koch's invitation for a return visit to East Prussia. I wanted every indication I could get of the timing of the Nazi programme, and I knew Erich Koch was the most likely person to help me. Bill gave the green light. I flew to Berlin and we flew straight on together to Königsberg. Bill told me Rosenberg was busy down south anyway, tidying up the rape of Austria, so I did not try to contact him—especially after our formal farewell at Nuremberg in 1937.

Koch came to meet us at the airport; he was his normal friendly self, but I was surprised at the lack of his usual bouncing energy. We dined quietly in the hotel which was now full of the military, mostly brass hats. Koch promised that he would take us for a few days' trip through the Masurian Lake district—away from the army! He had realised the strange beauty of these long, narrow, deep green waters which lay between steep pine-clad hills, the trees running down to the water's edge. I have seen some of the same sort of scenery on the Wanganui River in New Zealand, but instead of the pale greenery of the tree-ferns here was nothing but the deep blue-green of pines reflected in the still waters. There was a wonderful stillness everywhere.

Erich Koch had put up nice clean little hotels here and there by the lake-sides and had made plans to open up the area as a holiday centre; I think he found a measure of peace in these quiet surroundings—I know I could have. One could go endlessly from one lake to another, sometimes direct through narrow gorges, at others through a modern lock which had replaced some old rapids.

It was a fisherman's paradise, too. The fish was a cross between a fresh sardine and a brown trout, quite unsophisticated but a good fighter. I think it tasted best smoked over a fir-cone fire, a trick I had also learned with trout on the shores of New Zealand's lakes.

Did I think the English tourist would come to East Prussia? 'Yes, of course they would—well, sometime perhaps in the future.' What a waste of good holiday material that was.

We spent several days in these peaceful surroundings and it was here that Koch unburdened himself. Evidently plans were now well advanced for the great drive east and East Prussia was, of course, going to be in the thick of it. What was going to happen to *all* that he had done for his people? Now there was nothing but flocks of generals swarming all over his beloved East Prussia, digging here; cutting down forests; building aerodromes and masses of concrete this and concrete that; tunnelling; laying railways which were useless to his own plans. The whole thing was heartbreaking.

He did not know which he disliked the most, the Russians or the generals; and to prove his point he took us round by some of these massive earthworks on our way back to the capital. One of these was destined to be Hitler's Headquarters for the Russian Campaign, and it was here he nearly died when the Army tried to assassinate him in 1944. The military were certainly spoiling the countryside. The timing of all this coincided with other indications that, by 1938, Hitler's and the Army's plans had been finalised. I found Koch looking a little sideways at me now and again, as if he knew that we were both going to be in for trouble.

I asked him how long he was to be burdened with these Army

people. He smiled and said, 'That is in the nature of a leading question, but in my own opinion it will take at least three years to complete all their construction. By that time my country will probably sink under the sea from sheer weight of concrete.' So it was to be 1941 at the earliest in the east.

On our way back along one of the rather narrow roads there was a repair job being done, no doubt to carry some of the heavy lorries now crawling over the countryside. The whole scene reminded me of my boyhood—piles of broken hard stone being spread by hand and rolled in by a real old-fashioned steam roller. There was no room to pass. We waited for a while and when the steam roller driver just went on with his work Erich Koch got out and had a word with him. No dice—the old moustached driver just told him, *Gauleiter* or not, he was going to finish the job before moving out of the way. Erich Koch came back laughing. He turned to me and said, 'Now that is what I like to see, it is almost English. There is far too little independence amongst us Germans.' It was just another side of Koch's character.

I had a lot of time for Erich Koch as a man. He was not a racialist, but a true reformer, and boy! did the Prussians need reforming. He loathed the Communists, their genocide, their propaganda and their Secret Police State.

The Russians took him prisoner and kept him shut up for a number of years after the end of the war. They finally shot him, I guess because he was inflexible in his determination not to serve them.

14

'Haut Espionnage'

Back from East Prussia I found that good and reliable information coming out of Germany was being seriously curtailed. I decided to go and see my French opposite number in Paris.

Georges Ronin and I had got to know each other's views and thoughts extremely well over the years and in view of Rosenberg's disclosures I was not altogether surprised when I noticed a little uneasiness in our work now. He, of course, knew about my visits to Germany and he now began stressing caution. This was most unlike him. So loyal was he to his own Service chiefs that it was not until the beginning of the phoney war that he finally intimated to me that there appeared to be some leakage going on in high places. I, in turn, never told him of Rosenberg's list—it would have hurt him too much—but I had had my warning from Rosenberg and assured Georges I should not be going back to Germany.

Hitherto, I had been able to keep a private eye on German Air Force development. Expansion had been so rapid and thorough that many people in this country would not believe it. They should have done.

New methods were now obviously necessary to get our information, especially the sites and capacity of new aerodromes in the west. Georges Ronin and I discussed our troubles at some length. He was growing more and more dissatisfied with the general trend of affairs in France. The French General Staff, even though they were our allies, would give us no accurate or definite information about their own readiness beyond vague waves towards the Maginot Line.

Georges had fitted an enormous and ancient wooden camera

into a very old aeroplane which was flown up and down the Rhine by a civil pilot, an old pal of Georges'. The camera was operated by a splendid old man with a flowing beard who was normally a portrait photographer in Paris. They managed to keep track of some of the fortifications on the German side of the river. Couldn't this sort of exercise be profitably extended?

Now I myself had been shot down over the enemy lines in France during World War One. I had been a Scout pilot and had managed to get along reasonably well in dog-fights on normal patrols, but the army had an insatiable appetite for photographs of the enemy's activities. The rather slow photographic aircraft were fitted with hand-operated cameras which used heavy plates instead of film and could not take a picture above a few thousand feet. In order to cross the enemy lines, these aircraft had to be escorted by scouts, or fighters, as we now call them, whose job it was to protect them from attack by enemy fighters. The Germans, not unnaturally, did not like their positions being photographed so often, especially before a major operation. In consequence, losses on these missions were enormous.

I had a lucky escape, which is another story, but the methods used seemed to me at the time to be unnecessarily risky and totally unimaginative—always the same procedure: the rendezvous of the Scouts and Photographic Flight near enough to give the enemy plenty of warning, the long dive down to get within proper height of the target, the massed anti-aircraft fire, the swarms of enemy fighters, the dog-fights and the losses.

And yet in 1938, more than twenty years later, although the cameras and lenses had been vastly improved and automated, it was still not possible to take photographs above eight thousand feet because the camera lens got fogged with condensation from the cold air. This was, of course, suicide against modern anti-aircraft fire and fighters. What to do? One obviously could not cruise around over Germany at eight thousand feet taking pictures from a civil aeroplane, so Georges and I decided that we would each ask our bosses for a new, fast, high-flying commercial aeroplane on which we could try to develop a technique to get what we required.

We chose the American Lockheed 12A, a new and very handy

type of twin-engined executive aircraft. It had a heated cabin with room for five or six people, all very up-to-date by European standards at that time. Sir Cyril Newall, who was by now Chief of the Air Staff, agreed to the plan after surprisingly little persuasion and I managed, with the help of Imperial Airways, to get two aircraft over from the United States, one for Georges and one for me. Who was to fly the British one?

It was while I was looking around for the right type of aerial James Bond that I met Sidney Cotton.

Having got our aeroplane, we set out to try to devise some method of taking photographs over Germany without arousing suspicion. This meant a well hidden camera and operation from a much higher altitude than the eight thousand feet ordained so far.

Eventually it was Sidney Cotton, with two faithful helpers—Bob Niven, a young Canadian pilot, and Pat Conran, Sidney's very efficient secretary—who experimented with all the various cameras and gear that we could lay our hands on and found the answer to the problem. There were night-long sessions in Cotton's flat working out how the thing could be done and designing suitable frames from which to operate the camera; it was exciting, if strenuous.

We had bought some Leica cameras from Germany, the large type that hold a roll of film with two hundred and fifty exposures; they are generally used for such things as bird-watching or the growth of plants. Then a suitable hole had to be cut in the bottom of the aircraft and the area properly stressed. The special frame had to be made to take three Leicas, one pointing straight down and one on either side at an angle, so that we could get the maximum coverage; extra tanks had to be fitted and everything had to be secretly approved by the Air Registration Board.

We had to evolve some form of mechanism to operate the shutters. It could not be done individually by hand and the timing had to be just right to give the correct over-lap at heights which, we hoped, had hitherto been outside the scope of the R.A.F. No suitable equipment for these little cameras was available, it had to be made. This was a tricky mathematical question in which the R.A.F. helped us.

Now came the surprise. The cameras on their triple frame were fixed above the hole so that there was just enough room for a concealing shutter to be drawn across beneath the lenses and look like part of the outer skin of the aeroplane. When this shutter was open the warm air from the heated cabin was automatically drawn out of the hole and flowed over the lenses and, wonder of wonders, they did not fog up, even at a height of twenty thousand feet. It seemed almost too simple to be true. The possibilities were now limitless and the team went into action.

Bob Niven, who acted as co-pilot to Sidney Cotton, had done his short-service with the R.A.F. and was now ready to work for me. Pat Conran kept all the records and did the odd jobs. She actually operated the Leica cameras on some of the first experimental trips at high altitude up the West German coast.

The first attempts were remarkably good for such a small camera as the Leica, but the prints soon showed us that there was so much going on and so many details that needed to be more clearly seen, that we should have to do something better. The Leica prints were too small, and if enlarged too much became unreadable. This could be put right now that the technique was proved. The real joy was that it seemed obvious that the Germans had not tumbled to this idea because they raised no objection to a civil aircraft flying anywhere as long as it was flying high enough. They never did develop their air photography as we did, anyway.

Despite the limitation on their height of operation the R.A.F. had developed some very fine cameras during the inter-war period, together with just the sort of automatic operating gear that we wanted. All that we had to do now was to fit one of these large cameras into the hole and regulate the timing gear for the exposures to allow for the greater area of ground covered by one picture at high altitude. This was a small engineering job and, subjected to the warm air treatment just as the Leicas had been, the results were beyond expectation. Full appreciation must be expressed for the enthusiastic assistance given us by the R.A.F. photographic section.

Our first full-scale experimental trip was fixed up between Georges and me. It was to be a flight around the Mediterranean. Sidney Cotton was supposed to be a business executive interested in film locations and Bob Niven was his pilot. They flew the aircraft to Malta non-stop, and from there used the French Air Bases of Algiers and Bizerta. I don't think there was any Italian aerodrome, barracks, naval base or other object of military interest in Southern Italy, the Eastern Mediterranean and North Africa which was not faithfully recorded in the greatest detail by those splendid cameras in early 1939.

These results gave us the green light but they were also a little embarrassing to the Air Ministry which had, at that time, only a very small organisation for the interpretation of Aerial Photographs which was quite inadequate for the careful study and evaluation of such masses of photographic detail as we could now produce. Nor was it easy to train men and women in the art of photographic interpretation in a matter of weeks.

However, it was thanks to the Mediterranean mission that the Air Ministry were forewarned of what was to come, and they set about the job of Photographic Intelligence with some urgency. We were now able to obtain all the necessary cameras and equipment that we needed from the R.A.F., the R.A.F. marks were all filed off, and then Cotton and Niven were ready to go places.

The opening in the Lockheed's belly was very carefully hidden by a sliding panel which was operated from the cockpit and could not be opened from the outside. The camera was boxed in beneath the cabin floor and camouflaged to look like a spare fuel tank. As a try-out Sidney Cotton flew the aircraft into Berlin several times without taking any photographs just to see if the Germans would search the aircraft for such things. If they had discovered the camera they would have found nothing on the films and the result would not have been fatal. As it happened they never bothered. I think the fact of Sidney Cotton being an Australian flying an American aircraft helped.

It was on one of his flights to Germany, to the Frankfurt Air Rally, that my old acquaintance Kesselring, always a keen pilot, asked Cotton for a flight in this new aeroplane. They had not seen many of these small American executive aeroplanes in Germany at that time. Cotton offered to fly him around and let him take a hand at the controls. Kesselring was so tickled at the opportunity to fly this very handy machine that Cotton let him carry on for some time so that the trip included a flight up the Rhine, over most of the new aerodromes in the area.

I particularly wanted to see what progress had been made on these aerodromes since I was last there. It was typical of Cotton's nerve that, despite the presence of the great Kesselring in the aeroplane, the opportunity was too good to be missed. Cotton switched on the camera and the green light showing the continuity of exposures began to click on and off on the dashboard. Kesselring was intrigued but accepted the explanation that it was a device to show the petrol flow to the engines. The photographs were excellent.

I realised at the time that we had made a remarkable break-through in aerial photography and was able to envisage its possibilities in the coming conflict. The extent to which the system was finally developed, both by our own Royal Air Force and the Americans, meant that this highly accurate form of high espionage proved one of the major sources of intelligence during the war. The story of the full development of aerial photography during World War Two has been admirably told by 'Babs' Babington Smith in her book *Evidence in Camera*. There is little doubt that the air spy was also the forerunner of the methods now used for the maintenance of peace.

The development after the war of the well-known American U-2 High Spy aircraft which virtually covered the world, supplied the technique for the Satellite Spies which keep the surface of the globe under close observation at all times. As yet we cannot photograph the thoughts and intentions of over-ambitious demagogues. These are as important today as they were in Hitler's 'thirties. The human spy still has a job to do.

15

Peace and War

Baldwin had gone after the Abdication, admitting that he was never very well up in Foreign Affairs anyway. Chamberlain succeeded him. Enough has been written of that unfortunate man. That he was arrogant and thought he knew how to deal with Hitler were, I believe, true, and yet he seemed happy to put his head in the same old sand hole. He came out of it in September 1938 to do a quick sell-out or 'act of appeasement' of Czechoslovakia, but now the sand was running out. His reasoning may have been influenced by a well-founded and growing conviction that France would let us down. Intelligence reports had been hinting at this and I myself had had proof of it in Berlin. I believe there were several Francophiles in the Cabinet who would not believe it; nevertheless, I believe it was this underlying fear which induced Chamberlain to go to Munich to meet Hitler and Mussolini, and to try to work out some way of avoiding an immediate war over Czechoslovakia.

I don't think that, after their first meeting, Chamberlain trusted Hitler an inch. He must have discovered that the Nazis were playing for time as much as he was. They were not yet ready for war, but they needed the Czech arms factories, and a defendable buttress in the south-east against any surprise from that quarter.

It has been said that Chamberlain was literally pushed into making the 'Peace in our time' declaration in the heat of the paper-waving moment and against his better judgment. This I can believe of this rather too meticulous politician. Whatever anyone says about Munich, it gave us an almost breathless breathing space of twelve months in which to catch desperately at the lost moments of the past five years.

The story of the last two years before World War Two is the story of the Government in London being either utterly unwilling or unable to see the wood from the trees. The whole wood of the basic policy of the Germans had been put before them: massive rearmament, the determination to become a world power alongside the British Empire and America; the overlordship either politically or, if necessary, militarily of Europe, except Britain; and, finally, the great conquest of the Russian Communists.

This was the wood; these were the stakes of the game we had to play, a game we should have tried to win with all the brilliance of a master chess player. Instead we bumbled and stalled our way through meaningless treaties and bits of paper, dramatic meetings on unattainable objectives—the trees which seemed to blind the Government to the real and relentless objectives of the Nazis.

I still maintain that instead of engendering feverish and useless diplomacy over each successive Nazi move—the re-occupation of the Rhineland, the occupation of Sudetenland and the move into Austria—we should have tackled the wood at its roots.

What did we really want? Surely the destruction of the two most disruptive forces of the twentieth century—Nazi-ism and Communism. Could we have kept out of the 1939 war and still preserved our lives and liberty, and that of our friends in Europe who depended on us? Could we have better served the cause of freedom both for the little nations and the German Jews by using the only real weapon in our armoury, our neutrality, in return for non-aggression by Hitler in the West and for the eventual freedom of Poland and the Jewish Community, and, by so doing, have turned Hitler's Army eastwards from the start? What hope would there have been that Hitler would have kept his word? If there was one thing Hitler dreaded it was another war against Britain. He would have fallen for the bait, I feel sure, and been content to rely on the conquest of Russia to ensure him the over-lordship of Europe later. In any case the fate of Poland and the Jews could hardly have been worse.

Those nurtured on the balance of power in Europe argued that if Germany was once in a position to organise the Russian masses it would be the end of this mythical balance and of freedom for all of us; and besides, our honour would not allow us to abandon even temporarily those smaller nations who relied on our aid. What aid? We had seen the Baltic States swallowed by Russia, we had raised no finger at the rape of Austria and we had sold Czechoslovakia down the drain at Munich. I do not believe that any foreign nation can 'conquer' Russia, or, at least, keep her conquered. Russia, like China, simply absorbs conquerors or freezes them out, and a Russo–German conflict in 1940 would, in my opinion, have resulted in early German victories followed by a long-drawn-out resistance, culminating in a stalemate of exhaustion which would have made both sides ready to accept the Atlantic Treaty.

What were the real facts? All indications were that France had not the will to fight. There would be a show of resistance at the Maginot Line but there was no real chance of stopping the Germans coming round the northern end. France had misled us about her real military strength; she had no more than twenty divisions to combat a German *Blitzkrieg*; her air force was in a worse state than ours; and some at least of her top men were unreliable.

America had been assiduously wooed by the Nazis; a large section of the population and the Press were definitely Germanophile. The Germans had every reason to suppose America would stay out of the war in Europe. They proved right until Pearl Harbour and Winston Churchill persuaded Roosevelt that the war was global.

Our own Government had obstinately refused to face up to the whole problem. They seemed to be waiting for some miracle to get them out of the mess. They knew we could not stop the conquest of the European continent, so of what use then, other than pure provocation, was a defence pact with Poland and Rumania? It was completely hypocritical, but it slammed the door to any other course but war. I believe it was the result of pressure on the Government by those who wanted to see us in a war to destroy Hitler.

Could we have played Hitler along with some indication of our terms for neutrality until he was forced to make his pact with Russia? Even if Hitler had some hopes of our neutrality it would have been natural that the German Army should plan to protect their Eastern Front whilst they dealt with the West. The bare-faced absurdity of a pact with Russia fooled no one, but it did mean that the Germans had to occupy their half of Poland quickly in order to prevent the Russians taking the whole country. This may well have been one of the reasons for starting the war against Poland six months before they were ready to come westward. Also, they probably wanted to see whether, at the eleventh hour, we should really decide to fight them.

On the Russian side, too, the German pact was useful. Russia was not unaware of the Nazi hatred—a clash was bound to come sometime—but it was far better the Germans should wear themselves out in Europe first and, anyway, if Russia could occupy a large slice of Poland with German consent it would keep the original battlefields that much further from Russian soil. Meanwhile it gave Russia the same sort of breathing space that Munich gave to us, not that Stalin made much use of it.

The Russo–German Pact was the psychological moment when we could have struck our bargain and there could have been a minute in history which would have changed for the better the face of the world for many generations to come.

The Japanese would no doubt have had a go, but, with the whole might of America and our own substantial help in south-east Asia, they would not have got very far. In the event, the Bomb would have given the Western Democracies the authority to impose on the worn-out dictatorships the *Pax Atlantica*.

The Russians, like good chess players, plan their moves some years ahead. Could we have indulged in a little chess and pulled it off? As it was, we were committed to the apparently uncalculated risks of going to war with little better than our bare fists, and of sending an expeditionary force to France when every trained man, gun, tank and aeroplane was vitally necessary to the defence of this island, knowing that France was already a broken reed. We could not even go into a neutralised Belgium to cover the open flank of the Maginot Line; risks which, but for the inspired leadership of one man, the valour of the little boats at Dunkirk, the shining sacrifices of the Few in the air, and the brilliance of a Back-room boy and his radar team, would have led to absolute disaster for this country.

Peace and War

In March 1939 the Nazis seized those parts of Czechoslovakia (Bohemia and Moravia) which they had not been given under the Munich pact. There was ample evidence coming out of Germany that the Army was preparing to bring forward their operations 'to rectify the Danzig corridor position' in September 1939. And now the British Government, without any means of backing up a military threat, resorted to a diplomatic one: they made a Defence Pact with Poland. This finally closed the door and set us on a collision course.

Those of us who could made plans to take a last holiday, with a deadline for everybody to be back in London by mid-August.

I spent a week in the Alps above Chamonix where a party of French Air Scouts, boys of sixteen or seventeen, were studying air currents in the mountains. They played happily with their balloons and did not appear to have the slightest idea of what was in store for them. The Maginot Line complex had made them absolutely complacent. I went on to Normandy in order to be a little nearer home, and flew back to Heston in the Lockheed from Dinard.

And now, at the eleventh hour, Germany and Russia signed their ten-year non-aggression pact—we had been sold down the river for a change.

A few months earlier I had got permission from the Chief of Air Staff to buy an additional small single-engined three-seater Beechcraft aeroplane which Bob Niven used to fly and I used for communication work. It was from this aircraft that a fearless amateur photographer, who used to provide us with passport photographs genuine or otherwise, flying with Bob Niven along the Dutch coast at twenty-five thousand feet, took the only available pictures of the German Fleet at anchor in the Elbe just twenty-four hours before war was declared. They were shot at by German fighters but managed to get home with the goods. Admiral Godfrey, at that time the Director of Naval Intelligence, was relieved and delighted. This was first blood.

Cotton himself had flown off to Berlin in the Lockheed without my permission and was waiting hopefully in Berlin on some wild scheme of bringing about a meeting between Goering and Halifax by flying Goering to London. Cotton could never resist playing politics and getting mixed up in situations he did not understand. I dared not contact him in Berlin to tell him it was hopeless and that he was to return at once—in any case communications were a bit dicey by then—but eventually he sensed things were too hot and only got out of Berlin with twelve hours to spare by special permission from Goering himself. As Cotton flew back at an arbitrary five thousand feet, he saw row upon row of dark green German bombers on the military aerodromes, their noses pointing towards Warsaw. I was glad to see the aircraft safely back; it was only a matter of hours now.

It was not until after the war that we learned that in November 1937 Hitler held a secret conference with the War Minister, Blomberg, and his three Chiefs of Staff and the Foreign Minister, and told them that he considered the time had come to start his wars in the West and the East before anyone woke up to realities and rearmed, that the war in the East must start by 1942, and the war in the West by 1938, if necessary!

No wonder I had found them all a bit tense on my last visit to Germany.

It has been said that the comment of the Foreign Office after the declaration of war in September 1939 was that it was satisfactory to know that the correct protocol had been accurately and faithfully carried out. There seems to have been left over from the Middle Ages an aura of solemn magnificence and grand occasion about declaring war, whereas in 1939 it was surely the simple admission of the failures of successive governments to deal with the German menace from the start.

The unearthly wail of the air raid sirens, a poor substitute to the Heralds' Trumpets, had proclaimed the new war. Another generation of Britain's 'Contemptible Little Army', tough, determined men backed up with a few tanks, guns, and bren-gun carriers, had 'safely arrived in France'. There was no *Tipperary*; someone had forgotten to write one.

Alas, the Admiral died after a short illness late in 1939. It was a cruel blow to us all; the man who fought for the recognition of the Nazi menace did not live to see its overthrow. His death was the end of a tradition that the Chief of M.I.6 should be an admiral; the end of an era, too—an era of individual leadership, with individual responsibility for the efforts of his team, and encouragement of individual initiative.

Colonel Stuart Menzies, who had acted as deputy to the Admiral, temporarily took over a rather hot seat and in due course came to a compromise with the chiefs-of-staff and the other powers-that-were to retain the job, but now much of the responsibility was to be invested in committees. Stuart Menzies had a difficult time for a while but the production of an ever-increasing flow of information helped him to keep other claimants for his job at bay.

There was an atmosphere of distrust in France during that frozen winter of the phoney war in 1939–40. It was not easy for British personnel to visit areas under purely French control. I had to do so for a number of reasons and found that a large piece of notepaper headed with 'H.M.G.', a few words of *laissez passer*, a length of scarlet ribbon and the seal of a 'Vat '69' whisky bottle, plus a scrawled signature, gave me the freedom I required!

The Photographic Development Unit—the 'Cotton Circus' as it was called—was duly made legal and taken over by the R.A.F. The work of the first Spitfires fitted with a camera in the wing was prodigious. During the 'phoney war' the Unit was stationed close to Meaux, whence comes that queen of cheeses, Brie. I used to visit the cheesery in the town and bring home one of those lovely large flat round delicacies whenever I could.

It was vital that if, and when, the hot war started, we should have up-to-date information on the size and length of the runways and in fact all useful information of all the Belgian aerodromes. But, due to the influence Hitler had over the King of the Belgians, Belgium was strictly neutral; they would not even give us the information we wanted; nor must we violate Belgian air space. It was obvious just how much the Nazis had the Belgians scared. However, no one noticed the pale blue Spitfires flying as silently as possible at thirty thousand feet. The British Government officially knew nothing of this and it was only when the Top Brass were presented with a neatly arranged book containing detailed photographs of every Belgian aerodrome that anyone knew what had gone on.

Bob Niven had had to go back to the R.A.F. and early in the war he was killed over the North Sea in a Beaufort. One of the other pilots, 'Shorty' Longbottom, who flew so many of the Spitfire sorties, died during test pilot work after the war. They were both pioneers who deserve a place in air history.

I think one of the most heart-breaking events right at the beginning of the hot war was the discovery by the Spy Planes of the massing of the German tanks and armour in the Ardennes, ready for the break-through round the corner of the Maginot Line. These concentrations were never bombed. Was it, perhaps, for fear of being the first to break the unwritten truce on bombing land targets, or was it that, thanks to the Baldwin Government, we neither had the bombers nor the bombs capable of destroying the tanks, and the Germans knew it?

When the hot war started in 1940 Georges Ronin took command of a French bomber squadron, and after the collapse of France he managed to get in touch with me and asked whether he would be more use in the United Kingdom with de Gaulle, or whether he should remain in France. From 1940 to 1942 he served in the Vichy Government as Principal Assistant to the puppet French Air Minister. All that time he and one of his faithful colleagues kept in touch with me in London; they were in constant danger of the firing squad.

Whoever planned for our ill-equipped British Expeditionary Force to advance too late into Belgium must have been a fan of King Canute. Inevitably the German tide just rolled on and it soon became evident that they were adopting the same plan as in 1914, but a much hotted-up version, and that in driving due west across France they would split the British from what remained of the French armies.

16

Hot War

One of the principal reasons for the success of the German *blitzkrieg* in 1940 was the devastating effect of their dive-bombers. I suppose that few commanders of any service had ever been subject to bombing by an apparently screaming demon pointing a large bomb directly at one as it hurtled down to complete one's obvious destruction. The potential effectiveness of this weapon was never taken seriously enough. There was no secret as to the use to which these squadrons would be put, or the numbers available. They had even been seen in operation at manoeuvres and when it came to the real thing their effect was deadly.

A French artillery officer (a pre-war colleague) told me after the war that during the defensive withdrawal of the French, when the artillery split up into single guns and occupied the small copses and plantations one sees dotted about the countryside in Northern France, not only did the dive-bombers spot them and knock them out but, to make matters worse, a large number of the boxes of ammunition contained only bricks; another result of Rosenberg's list.

Shortly after the fall of France I was dining with General Ismay. Discussion turned to what would really happen if England was invaded. 'Pug' Ismay described with some relish how he would enjoy sticking the new sticky bombs onto German tanks. I told him, I remember, that I could not believe it would really happen; in any case, I was probably on one of Rosenberg's lists as a possible *gauleiter* of Occupied Britain. Nevertheless, I acquired a Colt Automatic and made sure I could use it pretty accurately.

Ismay told me the simple story of Winston Churchill's last vain attempt to stop the French capitulation during the final stages of France's agony. The remnants of the French government had fled to Tours and it was to Tours, across war-torn France on a black night, that Winston Churchill and Ismay flew in a small transport plane. There was no one to meet them at Tours Aerodrome, everything was dark and deserted, but somehow they succeeded in getting a car to take them to the hotel where it was reported that Paul Reynaud, the French Prime Minister, was staying.

On a rather dingy red plush sofa they sat and waited while the French Prime Minister was persuaded to leave his bedroom in his dressing-gown and come and talk to them. In the ill-lit hall Winston Churchill again begged Reynaud to pull the French nation together and resist. But it was too late. The people and their leaders were already demoralised. It was two o'clock in the morning when Winston Churchill and General Ismay finally left Reynaud to return to a bed that had been kept warm for him.

There was not much darkness left for the flight back but it had to be risked. Neither of them spoke until they were once again safely airborne. Then Winston Churchill, tears in his eyes, said quietly: 'Well, we are all alone now.' Nor did they talk again until they landed.

I had met General Ismay in the hunting field before the war. Perhaps it was his unobtrusive fitness which enabled him to serve Churchill so well during the strenuous war years. It is, I think, well known that Churchill was not an early riser, but he had to have his papers early enough and those around him had to see he had them. On the other hand, at the other end of the day, he seldom went to bed before 2 a.m.

Often I had to telephone him at this hour and I have had the strangely uncanny feeling of listening to the Great Man thinking on the other end of the line. He was the only person with whom I have ever had this experience. I would give him some urgent information—there would be complete silence, but somehow I sensed what was going through his mind. The spell would only be broken when I got my instructions loud and clear and a 'ring me back when you've done this'—a lesson I never forgot when I myself wanted something done with no 'buts'.

Dunkirk. There is no doubt in my own mind that Hitler did not press the issue. This impression was soundly based on intelligence available at the time. It may be argued that his Priority Number One was the absolute defeat of the French and the belief that Britain would then ask for an armistice. I am certain that, despite the fact we had entered the war and sent a gallant army to inevitable defeat, Hitler still hoped for eventual co-operation from Britain in the years ahead. He certainly did not want a whole captive British Army in Germany.

When one looks back at the gamble our politicians and War Office took not only with the lives of the army but with the very existence of our country, and compares it with the gamble of neutrality I set out in a previous chapter which would also have given us time to really re-equip our armed forces, I cannot help feeling that history will pass a harsh judgment on our leaders of the 'thirties, despite the eventual American-British victory which killed one bloody eagle only to let loose the wolves of a bloodier Communism.

So many brilliant and detailed accounts have been written about the operations of the Allied Forces in World War Two that I propose only to highlight a few events where it seemed to me that Intelligence played its most successful roles and to give some impressions of the V.I.P.s whom I knew and worked with.

August 1940, and the focus was now on invasion. Information and photographs had shown us that the setting up of air loading bases on aerodromes in France and Holland was one of the main enemy preparations. Much emphasis was evidently being placed on air landings, supply by air of troops already landed, and air reinforcement. Meantime the build-up of those great continental river barges in the French and Dutch harbours was prodigious, but before the German generals would risk invading they had to have mastery of the air over the Channel.

The Battle of Britain was fought and won, as everyone knows, primarily by the men who kept our aircraft in the air, a handful of heroes who flew them, 'Stuffy' Dowding, and radar. Nevertheless, Intelligence also played a considerable part in this early warning system, and I kept a quick and personal contact with the Commander-in-Chief, Fighter Command.

The Germans were well behind us in the science of electronic echo-sounding and during those years before World War Two, while the brilliant scientist Robert Watson-Watt was working away in his wooden huts on the bleak Suffolk coast, no breath of his success was allowed to escape. When the hot war came nearer it was one of my vital jobs to find out whether the Germans knew anything about it.

As radar was a bit complicated, I asked for some scientific assistance. Sir Robert Watson-Watt, as he now is, and the late Sir Henry Tizard attached to my staff a young scientist, R. V. Jones, who was to make a name for himself in scientific intelligence. Great care had been taken to keep the smiling Wenninger completely ignorant of our success up to September 1939 and, as far as I know, the only sign that the Germans were at all interested in this sort of thing concerned the Navy. The Germans continued to carry out a continual search for what they called the 'ASS-Deck' of a destroyer—submariners will appreciate the reference.

One satisfaction during the Battle of Britain was to visualise Goering, in his grand new Air Ministry in Berlin, red in the face and blowing sky-high all his staff because no one understood how, with a mere handful of fighters, we managed to locate and attack their great formations whenever they crossed the French coast.

It is commonplace now to see the 'ops room' on film or television, but during the Battle of Britain they were grim and efficient, despite the apparently light-hearted directions to the pilots in the air about angels and bandits. The calm of 'Stuffy' Dowding, on whose shoulders lay the fate of the nation; the swift precision of the girls at the plotting tables, desperately tired though they were; the controllers' eyes dark with lack of sleep; the whole radar set-up—this was the greatest secret weapon yet. And now, when we see vast radar screens covering the whole northern hemisphere, it is well to remember those tireless little stations spread along the South Coast in 1940, working the clock round.

Although we often managed to get two or three hours' notice of the earlier mass air raids, such as the first daylight raid on the Port of London, and the great blitz on the city, in general I could only tell Stuffy Dowding when and not where a big raid would take place. Nevertheless in those cases where Goering gave his flamboyant orders for the destruction of England, even a few hours' notice was vital to alert all the A.A. fire and ambulance services and to start a decoy fire away from the target.

How well I remember the agonising hours before the raid on Coventry. The Prime Minister himself had to take the decision as to whether or not the population should be told. He rightly decided that such action would cause pandemonium and probably more deaths than if people stayed in their cellars. As soon as I had heard his decision I went down to my cottage just out of London to the west and as I stood in my garden and counted the aircraft going north with the characteristic throb-bump-throb-bump of their engines I offered a silent prayer for the people of Coventry.

If the government had left the country unprepared for the German air assault, Intelligence, Radar and the R.A.F. did their best to remedy the situation.

It was only in 1941 that the Germans finally tumbled to the fact that we must have some means of detection they did not know about and started to experiment on their own account. By that time they had seen, and no doubt photographed, our own radar stations on the coast and had some idea of what it was all about. In due course they set up a station at Bruneval, on the coast of Brittany, and it was R. V. Jones who was the instigator of the raid which brought back the vital bits of the first German radar so that we could study them here and see how far they had got.

It was interesting to see the part played by aerial photography in this operation. Aerial photographs were taken again and again of the site of this German station at Bruneval, and an exact model was built up at the Photographic Interpretation Unit, giving a miniature replica of the area of coast concerned. The raiding parties were carefully briefed and exercised with the model so that everyone knew and would recognise the area and would know exactly how to go about it. This was, I think, one of the first times that such models were used with such great success.

Late September 1940, and the sirens wailed their now nightly warning soon after dusk. Goering had switched his air raids away from our aerodromes to our cities, a move which probably saved the R.A.F., but when even these daylight raids proved too costly he switched again to night bombing.

The mass of invasion barges had been moved down from Holland and moored in their hundreds opposite our coasts. Each day they were faithfully photographed. Despite all the evidence of the ostentatious build-up of the invasion fleet, I could never really convince myself that the invasion was going to take place. I knew that Hitler would not want to waste either the time or the troops in this adventure; his mind must have already turned eastward. The generals would certainly not look forward to a sea invasion—German soldiers for generations have been trained to cross rivers in great land campaigns but they do not like the sea; invasion by sea is not in their text books.

By now the British, who should have been cowering helpless on an undefended island, were supposed to ask for peace. In fact, we were supposed to ask for peace when France fell. I could imagine the infuriated Goering being the scapegoat for the doubts which must now be being voiced by Keitel and Jodl, with Hitler, I fancied, smiling to himself.

It was a warm night for late September. There had been a little drizzle, the noise of the A.A. guns and bombs was inter-mittent. At about midday information had been received that the Germans had given orders to dismantle the aircraft loading ramps on a Dutch aerodrome. The information was immediately passed to the Chiefs of Staff and I put a note on a copy to Winston Churchill explaining just what this meant. He called a meeting of the Chiefs of Staff, together with my Chief and myself, for that evening in the war room deep under Whitehall.

Everyone had been under such a strain during the past few weeks that it was not surprising to feel a sudden breaking of the tension. The full meaning of this information was explained to the meeting: it confirmed Operation Sea-Lion was off. The generals had funked it, and I am sure they had Hitler's full agreement. Churchill was beaming and there were controlled smiles on the faces of the great. 'Pug' Ismay's grin showed that he had overcome his desire to throw sticky bombs at German tanks.

Winston Churchill suggested we should all go up and have a

breath of fresh air. The misty rain had cleared since we had been down below and now, as we emerged from behind the tall concrete barrier shaped like a huge folding screen which guarded the entrance to the War Room, the boom and crack of bombs and A.A. guns had risen to a crescendo. I saw General Ismay trying to persuade the Prime Minister not to go out in front of the barrier, but the red glow in the sky was too much for him.

Would that I could have captured the scene on canvas: the Great Man in his boiler-suit and tin hat stood, flanked by his three Chiefs of Staff and General Ismay, both hands on his stick in front of him, his chin thrust out, cigar between his teeth; and just across St. James' Park, Carlton House Terrace ablaze. The brilliant glow of the orange-white flames silhouetted every detail of the great trees in the Park and, as it played on his features, dimmed the light of Churchill's cigar. The roar of the fire echoed round the Horse Guards' Parade.

Before he turned away I heard him say: 'We'll get the —— for this.' It was one of those piquant moments of history.

It was one of those three Chiefs of Staff, Lord Newall, who gave me my job, who backed me with aeroplanes for the photographic missions, and gave me his trust despite my difference of opinion with the Government over German air rearmament. His courtesy and understanding were unfailing. I last saw him when I lunched with him at Government House in New Zealand where he was, for some time after the war, a distinguished Governor-General.

17

Barnes Wallis

It has been said that Hitler and his Staff were so pre-occupied with the development of secret weapons that would 'win the war' for them that they neglected the conventional equipment required by the army and air force. This may have been true to a certain extent, but, in point of fact, had the V-1 and the V-2 weapons been ready a year earlier things might well have been very difficult for us in the United Kingdom. Over here it was an axiom of the British Staffs not to waste too much time or effort on some of the hare-brained schemes for winning the war which poured from the country retreats of enthusiastic inventors. There was one scheme, however, which should have merited closer attention from the start.

So much has been written about Barnes Wallis and the Dam Busting Bomb that I do not propose to enlarge on the fruitful stages of this affair, but it might be of interest to give an accurate account of the very earliest stages of this invention by quoting some of the correspondence which I had with those people who I knew would eventually have to take decisions on this project and which, in fact, did obtain the first recognition of Wallis's ideas.

But let us begin at the beginning.

It was after a not unusually excellent lunch in the late autumn of 1940 at the house of a very good friend, a highly successful City banker who has always taken an intense interest in all things aeronautical. He asked me if I would like to come down with him in his car to Effingham, in Surrey, for a chat, as he called it, with an interesting inventor and aeronautical scientist. He told me that this man had been the inventor of the geodetic system of construction of the Wellington bomber which was, after all, the most successful one in the early days of the war. My friend thought that we might have much in common; we did.

Barnes and Mollie Wallis still live in that same house looking out over the Effingham golf-links, somewhat enlarged now to accommodate the relays of visiting grand-children. Barnes eats no meat, nearly everybody in the house seems to play some sort of musical instrument; there is ever a delightful air of individual effort co-ordinated at mealtimes around mounds of good food. I count myself fortunate to have known Barnes and his family fairly well over the years.

As a result of our first meeting at Effingham I managed to get Barnes to lunch with me at the Royal Air Force Club shortly afterwards. The German bombers had just started dropping those five-hundred-pounders on London and many and curious were the stories of windows and walls being sucked inwards or outwards, roofs caving in and such-like, often in quite a different street from the actual burst of the bomb.

I suppose it had been principally due to the R.A.F.'s policeman-like duties in the Middle East that we had not, in fact, developed a large bomber or a large bomb during the inter-war years. It seemed, therefore, that we knew very little about the effect of bombs of five hundred pounds and upwards. Air Marshal Sir Victor Goddard had for a long time been advocating four-engined bombers to carry larger bombs, but this had never come off. Our bombing in the Middle East had been principally for punitive destruction of Arab villages or anti-personnel bombs and the like. The efficiency of our bombs had therefore been reckoned in blast value. It had evidently been decided, on this basis, that it was better to drop a number of small bombs to create a wider area of destruction by blast than confine the damage to a single large one. The German five-hundred-pound bombs were causing destruction out of all proportion to their blast effect, especially since they usually exploded deep inside a building.

Barnes' scientific brain was beginning to work on this matter and he was determined to find out *why* all these strange things happened. Nor did he take long to do so. The answer lay in the great efficiency of the anti-submarine depth-charge detonated under water. This did not destroy by means of blast; it did so by means of a shock-wave which was transmitted by the water itself. Nobody seemed to have thought that the air, or the ground, could do the same thing. Here, then, was the answer to the destruction wrought by the big German bombs—the shock wave.

As I got to know Barnes better we had lunch together more frequently, either at the Club or at the house of our mutual friend. I was able to give him certain information about the effect of these large bombs and he, in his turn, was making an exhaustive study of the effect of shock-waves. His keen mathematical mind had worked out endless possibilities with regard to the size of bomb and the depth of penetration and the probable results of the explosion. And now nothing would do but that I must summon the Air Staff to adopt his plan for a large penetrating bomb without delay.

In those very early days Barnes could not envisage the possibility of anybody not falling in with his ideas at once. But the Air Staff were fully engaged in building up the Air Force after the losses of men and aircraft earlier on. Anyway, I was well aware that half-baked untried schemes had little chance of a hearing at this critical stage of hostilities, especially where new types of construction were involved. Nevertheless, I was anxious to get some reaction as to the sort of welcome such a scheme might receive.

Due to my job I was not necessarily bound by the same orthodox methods as other government departments. I had a friend in the Prime Minister's Office who I knew would get a reaction from 'Prof' Lindemann, as he then was. The reply was not too discouraging:

Prime Minister   10 Downing Street,
                                                                      Whitehall.
                                                              5th July, 1940

My dear Fred,
    I have not only read your interesting paper on the ultimate aim of bombing warfare but have consulted certain goodwilled experts without disclosing your identity.
    The view held is that such a project as you describe could not come to fruition until 1942, even if then. This may not be a complete bar, since the war may still be going on in that year.
    It is suggested, however, that if the plan is to be put into effect

in a reasonable period the best thing to do is to take it up with the Boeing Company, or some other American firm used to work of this type.

Thus modified there is no reason why your plan should not be a perfectly practicable one. . . .

Yours ever,
(Sgd.) Desmond Morton.

Barnes was impatient and disappointed but I finally persuaded him that nothing but a full reasoned study on the subject would have any chance of success, and so it was that some seven months later, in March 1941, the paper was produced. It was brilliant and showed, with many accurate calculations and drawings, the damage that could be caused to German underground oil installations, canals, docks, railway sidings, etc. by the use of a long ten-thousand-pound bomb with a reinforced nose dropped from a great height, penetrating deep into the earth before exploding. The destruction would be purely by means of the shock wave and the result would be something like a small earthquake. Obviously Barnes had put a great deal of research into his paper and I duly forwarded it to both the Air Staff and to Professor Lindemann at No. 10 Downing Street.

The reply from the Air Ministry was courteous but pointed out, as I rather expected, the great difficulty of meeting existing commitments in the air without embarking on any new project, especially one of this magnitude. Professor Lindemann, on the other hand, was, I was told, still of the opinion that no such bomb or aircraft capable of carrying it would be built in time to be used in World War Two. Barnes was completely dejected.

However, I managed to get him an introduction to Lord Beaverbrook who was at that time at the Ministry of Aircraft Production and, as a result, a further meeting was arranged with the Director of the Scientific Research Department. At the Director's request I sent him a short aide-memoir as follows:

To: The Director of Scientific Research,
The Ministry of Aircraft Production,
London, S.W.1.

14th April, 1941

Dear D.S.R.,

I enclose the details about the new large aircraft which the Germans appear to be constructing in Czechoslovakia. This information comes from a usually reliable source. I endeavoured to obtain copies of the blue prints of this aircraft, but in the present circumstances I fear it will not now be possible to get them out of Czechoslovakia.

Thank you for ringing me up. I feel I should have put you in the picture before. I confess to having been responsible for inaugurating, last July, the enquiry into the potentialities of the very large bomb. I was prompted to do so by the trend of development in Germany and U.S.A. . . .

As you know, the Minister instructed Tedder to give all assistance and after 8 months the Wallis report was produced. I understand the obvious necessity of ensuring that the conclusions reached in the report are not based on 'moonshine'. At the same time, exhaustive enquiries made during the past 8 months, together with the interesting discussion at your meeting, appear to me to make it evident that neither the actual effect of a 10 ton bomb can at present be accurately predicted, nor the suggested effect disproved. . . .

May I take this opportunity of congratulating you on the choice of Dr. R. V. Jones as my scientific assistant. I am sure you will agree that although his work during the past twelve months has not always been palatable to some departments, it has been of outstanding merit and value to all concerned.

Yours sincerely,
(Sgd.) F. Winterbotham.

After a long meeting at which Dr. Pye endeavoured to obtain from numerous scientists some confirmation of the figures of the report, it was pointed out to Barnes how difficult it would be—at the existing state of our explosive development—to detonate a bomb of some fifteen feet long so that the whole length of the bomb detonated at the same instant, a feature which was necessary if a shock wave of the intensity required was to be obtained.

Barnes retired back to his home in Surrey. It was some weeks before I heard of him again. Then one day he rang up and suggested that we might meet; he thought he had got something interesting to tell me.

In those days Barnes had not had very much publicity beyond that accorded to him for his invention of geodetic construction for aeroplanes. He was rather shy and diffident with strangers and because of this was often thought to be somewhat inarticulate. Amongst friends, however, there are few men I have met who could make one understand more lucidly than he, what he was driving at, and now, when he arrived, I noticed a certain suppressed excitement; before we had had time to sit down, he started:

'My dear boy, don't you see, the obvious solution is to have a spherical bomb. Detonated from the centre, the explosion will reach all points of the surface at precisely the same moment.'

'But surely, Barnes,' I said, 'a round bomb won't penetrate deeply enough to do any real damage with a shock wave.'

'I don't know,' Barnes replied. 'Do you think the Air Ministry would have any data on that subject, I wonder?'

Well, there was nothing for it. I then and there rang up my friends in the department of the Air Ministry concerned and I put the question to them: 'What would be the effect of dropping a large spherical bomb from about ten thousand feet?'

There was a chortle from the other end of the phone and my contact said: 'My dear chap, it would bounce along like a football. No accuracy at all—absolutely no accuracy. Anything else you want to know?' I thanked him and rang off.

'Barnes,' I said, 'it would bounce along like a football.'

There was a long pause. 'But my dear boy,' said Barnes, 'splendid! Splendid! Don't you see?' And before we could have any further conversation he gathered up his briefcase—he never wore a hat, anyway—and left.

Of course, I didn't see, but a few days later he was on the phone again. Could I, by any chance give him the drawings of the new Lancaster bomber that was due to come into service shortly. It was a four-engined version of the twin-engined Manchester which had proved a failure. The drawings were still secret but I did arrange to show them to Barnes the following week. It was on a Monday and Barnes was really excited.

He told me how he had spent the whole of Sunday shooting a glass marble with a catapult at the surface of a tin bath full of water. He had been helped by Mary and Christopher, two of his children, who had had a wonderful time, and there was no doubt about it—there must be a law of ricochet, if he could find it.

I did not, at first, quite follow what he was up to; and then he explained: 'How about bouncing the bomb along the surface of the water against their dams and harbours.'

Close examination of the Lancaster drawings showed that a

large spherical bomb could be carried. Barnes was happy; he had at last got something he could get his teeth into. Again I begged him to come up with a properly baked pie—no under-cooked blackbirds, please! From now on we were in constant touch.

The first essential was to establish some sort of law relating to weight, size, speed and dropping height of a sphere, to the length of bounce, and now, for several days, Barnes with one or two helpers, including his own children, spent the daylight hours firing wooden balls of different weights and sizes from a catapult along the water tanks of the National Physical Laboratory at Teddington.

Both Barnes and I had managed to get Sir Henry Tizard interested in the project, and although he had recently been replaced in his job by Professor Lindemann, nevertheless his help was very welcome in getting the use of the National Physical Laboratory. Tizard came down to watch the experiments and after two days of hard work a pattern of bounces began to emerge; finally, after Barnes had managed to put a back-spin on the ball, he got near enough in his calculations to predict with considerable accuracy what eventually happened at the Möhne Dam. But this was still a long way off.

Testing with models was all very well, but if this project was to come to anything in time, then all the paraphernalia of Ministry of Production agreement and authorisation for prototype manu-facture and test had to be gone through, and gone through quickly. Although Barnes was one of the principal designers at Vickers Aviation and had all the facilities at hand for making and testing dummy bombs, he could not do anything without proper authorisation, so that the time was now ripe to put the whole project up once again to the Government.

As I have said, Barnes at that time was not at his best when up before a panel of strangers or at a meeting where he did not know everybody very well, and so I offered to act as his spokesman since I knew the ins-and-outs of government procedure. Fortunately, also, I knew Garro-Jones, later Lord Trefgarne, who was then Parliamentary Private Secretary to the Minister of Production.

A new Scientific Committee had just been set up under the Ministry with the duties of examining this sort of thing; so many projects were being brought forward that the Government wanted some authoritative scientific advice on them. The Chairman of this Committee was that charming scientist, Sir Thomas Merton.

I quote my Brief to Garro-Jones of 14th September, 1942:

SECRET AND PERSONAL

S.W.1.

14th September, 1942.

Dear Garro

"I attach the notes I promised concerning B. N. Wallis and his invention. . . .

Yours sincerely,

F. Winterbotham

G. M. Garro Jones, Esq.,
Parliamentary Secretary,
Ministry of Production, Great George Street, S.W.1.

Notes on the Work of Mr. B. N. Wallis

Airframe designer to Vickers Aviation.

Inventor of Geodetic Construction.

Designer of the Wellesley and the Wellington.

In March 1941, he put forward comprehensive proposals for the construction of a Stratosphere Bomber to carry 10 ton bomb, for destruction of Axis primary sources of power—coalmines, water power dams and oil refinery and storage plants by—utilisation of new and hitherto unrealised potentiality of 'shock wave' of large bombs.

The proposition was favourably viewed by Lord Beaverbrook, and its possibilities were admitted by a technical committee set up by Sir Henry Tizard to report on Wallis's paper. It was, however, turned down by the Air Staff, but in spite of this resulted in the formation of an 'Air Attack on Dams' Committee under the chairmanship of Dr. Pye (Director of Scientific Research of the Ministry of Air Production).

During 1941–1942, Wallis has continued to press forward with methods of destroying enemy water dams. It is considered that the question of the amount of damage which could be caused by the destruction of enemy water power has not been fully realised, for instance, the destruction of the Möhne dam at the head of the Ruhr

Valley would flood the valley, and put many factories out of action, thus saving much costly bombing: whilst the destruction of the hydro-electric power in Italy would cripple transport and industry throughout that country.

Experiments have shown that the destruction of large dams requires bombs at least of the size forecast by Wallis, and even larger when they are dropped in the usual way and explode in the water as near misses. This is presumably the reason why the project has not been favourably received by the Air Staff, but experiments have also shown that large dams can be destroyed by much smaller charges than those required above, provided that the charge is detonated in actual contact with the masonry of the dam on the water side at a considerable depth below the surface.

It is agreed that it is impossible to accomplish the second method by ordinary bombing, and Wallis has accordingly invented a 'surface torpedo' which when dropped by a low-flying aircraft will travel a considerable distance (estimated at about one mile) along the surface of the water.

The possibilities of this weapon seemed so great that I put Wallis in touch with Professor Blackett of the Admiralty over this subject and Blackett then arranged with Sir Henry Tizard for Wallis to be given facilities for further experiments.

This surface torpedo, or 'Rota-mine' as it has been called to conceal its real nature, has been taken up with enthusiasm by the Admiralty as it shows some prospect of revolutionising air–naval warfare, and every destroyer can be equipped with catapult apparatus capable of projecting Rota-mines along the surface of the water to distances of about three miles at an average speed of some 200 m.p.h. The Admiralty, however, deal only with the naval side, and although an aircraft is being equipped for Admiralty trials with small Rota-mines, no action is being taken regarding the other and major applications of this device, such as the destruction of dams and harbour works, etc.

It has, in fact, appeared that the official attitude throughout has been to prove that things *cannot be done* rather than to find out *how to do them.*

Conclusive proof that the largest dam in Europe could be effectively destroyed by a Rota-mine carrying an 8,000 lbs. charge, was obtained from a large-scale experiment in Wales last July. This size Rota-mine could be carried by any existing Stirling or Lancaster bomber, after suitable modification. Dr. Pye's Committee has not

even been called to meet to discuss this matter, and no action whatever is being taken to prepare plans for the adaptation of the necessary aircraft.

The Admiralty experiments are unlikely to be completed within
the next two months. Small scale experiments in the William Froude
Tank at the National Physical Laboratory have however demon-
strated the inventor's claims and no reason is seen for this experience
to be reversed in larger sizes.

If this new weapon is intelligently used, e.g., for simultaneous
attacks on all German capital ships and main hydro-electric power
dams, there is little doubt but that Italy could be brought to a
complete standstill, and that industry in Germany would be so
crippled as to have a decisive effect on the duration of the war.

To attain this result much preparation and careful planning are
clearly required, and meanwhile I repeat *nothing is being done*.

Garro-Jones was sufficiently impressed with my description of
this new project to fix a hearing with the Merton Committee. It
was, as a matter of fact, their first case and we had a long and
interesting examination. I was known as 'Wallis's Impresario'—
at any rate I was now getting used to the patter!

There were agonised weeks of waiting and then, at last, Wallis
was given the go-ahead, but Garro-Jones warned me that our
troubles had only just begun. The distribution of skilled men and,
even more, of precious materials was so tight and priorities were
so jealously guarded that even if the experimental project was
successful, full-scale manufacture was bound to run into snags.
However, for the time being at any rate, Barnes Wallis was
authorised to go ahead with the construction and testing of a
prototype of his bouncing bomb. At last I had succeeded in help-
ing Barnes get the project off the ground.

Barnes had always been a prodigious worker. I have watched
him cover sheet after sheet with complicated equations until my
own brain reeled; that, of course, was before the days of computers.
But now his calculated results and model tests gave him a growing
confidence and he seemed better able to measure up to the various
authorities with whom he had to argue. I knew that once he had
got used to the official approach he could explain his ideas and
requirements much more lucidly than I could. The time came

when he no longer needed his 'impresario'; anyway, my own work demanded all my time. I was, however, able to supply him with accurate air photographs of the target which proved invaluable.

The story from this point has been well told, both in the book *The Dambusters* and, more lately, by David Irving in his articles. The failure of the first tests at Chesil Beach, Barnes' perseverance, and the great result have all been faithfully recorded.

Barnes, the son of a parson, is one of the few scientists that I have run across who is a sincere Christian. His attitude towards science was, I think, best explained by an incident which occurred when he was trying to devise some method of taking a large number of electric leads through a very small hole.

'My dear boy,' he said, 'do you realise that the Almighty has arranged a system whereby *millions* of electric circuits pass up and down a single cord no bigger than my little finger, and each one most beautifully insulated. The spinal cord is an absolute marvel of electronics.'

I think it was working with Barnes that helped me to reconcile my own views of the Almighty and Evolution.

Perhaps it is because I have been lucky enough to travel and observe people in many corners of this earth, and have spent odd times in out-of-the-way places in Australia and Africa, that I have taken a special interest in a layman's view of evolution. Maybe also the stories of my grandfather who knew New Zealand in the days of the early settlers and of my uncle who bred the finest black horses in the whole of Southern Russia, whetted the appetite of my inherited wanderlust.

Whatever the cause, the effect has been a keen interest in the habits and customs of the various races who inhabit this world and an ever-increasing wonder at the way so many people who now exercise a new-found ability to articulate seem to think that human beings all over the rest of the world react in the same way to the problems of living as they do.

Climate seems to have played an important role in evolution and one can't help seeing the gap between those people who have evolved in a temperate climate, with their energy and stimulus to imagination, their curiosity and more balanced emotions on the one hand, and their less fortunate brothers who have had to contend with extremes of heat and cold. To see but one example, one has only to stay awhile in some remote village in Central Africa to realise the almost complete lack of ability to control the emotions. No 'British phlegm' here. After millions of years, love, hate, temper, grief, and joy are still not far removed from the animal kingdom, and wisdom is still a long way from a deeply inherited cunning, and yet some of the peoples of the Western hemisphere naively expect these ancient tribal races to settle down together like sophisticated western democracies after a few decades of white occupation has come to an end.

Friendly, happy and childlike as they are, the majority of Africans are not yet ready to discard their tribal inheritance.

Whatever the course of evolution has been I agree with Barnes Wallis that the delicate hand of the Almighty appears at every stage, guiding, improving and balancing the wondrous works which science is gradually unfolding, and, alas, in some cases claiming as their own discoveries.

I like to think that there is a simple explanation for the out-spread of the continents on this earth, and that when a blob of half molten earth flew off into space to become the moon, the hole it left filled with water. That we came by way of fish and mammal to the estate of homo—slightly sapiens—when it pleased the Almighty to give us a spirit, to guide our ever increasing wisdom; a digression, but one which perhaps gives some indication of my own character in so far as I try and get to the simplest possible base of a problem and not produce an 'absence of clear thinking' by getting cluttered up with irrelevant details.

Barnes and I usually celebrated any major advance in our plans with a lunch at the Royal Air Force Club, and it was on a sunny day in June 1943 that we and some members of our families had an extra good one on our return from Buckingham Palace. Barnes' C.B.E. was for dam-busting, my own for other reasons, but the fact that we had gone to get them together was a happy ending to that particular project.

Barnes and Mollie and their family usually took one of those strenuous holidays hiking in the Lake District, but after the war was finished my wife (whom I had met during the war) and I persuaded Barnes to come with us to Taormina, in Sicily. In the 'good old days' of 1946 a comfortable flying-boat put one down gently onto the calm waters of Mussolini's Mare Nostrum at Augusta, and thence one travelled by car to the little hotel on the beach at Taormina. There were few other people there except the local Sicilians. The sun and the sea and the welcome were really warm, and I like to think that the three-week lazy holiday we had there with Barnes did us all a lot of good. The only trouble was his passion for green figs!

Taormina had had an interesting history, as far as I was concerned, during the war itself. In 1943, before the Allied landing in Sicily, my old 'friend' Kesselring, then the Commander-in-Chief of the German forces in the Mediterranean, had established his headquarters in a hotel on the top of the hill at Taormina. The hotel had at one time been an old monastery but had been bought and converted by a German princeling. It was close to the great Greek amphitheatre; even today the acoustics of that ancient place are phenomenal. I know of few more moving experiences than to listen to Debussy's *Au Clair de Lune* with a full moon playing on the sea beyond the great pillars of the proscenium black against the sky.

But to go back to the hotel and its owner, Prince Mimi. We had discovered that Kesselring had established his headquarters there and the R.A.F. had made a most amazing raid on this target. They had dropped their bombs precisely on the one place in the hotel which contained the officers' mess. It was unfortunate for us, really, that Kesselring was away at the time; I am afraid a great many German officers perished in that raid, but it did the hotel very little damage and, as a result, the prestige of the R.A.F. amongst the Sicilians and the Italians was extremely high.

The local Sicilians started talking to me about the raid and when I admitted to having some knowledge of it they immediately introduced me to the owner as being the person who had dropped the bombs on his hotel during the war. The poor chap certainly went very red in the face but to his credit he did not say anything. The damage had been easily repaired after the war and the hotel was again in full swing, so he had not much to complain about as he was not there himself at the time of the bombing.

It was here in Taormina in 1946 that Barnes first described to me and Whitney Strait who was with us, the principles of the design of his swing wing aeroplane. I had known for some time that he had been working on such a design, and that he was not getting much encouragement. In the event it was to be another twenty years before his ideas were incorporated in an American military aircraft.

18

Recovery

What a dreary, damp, sleepless winter was that of 1940–41; the sirens screaming their nightly banshee warning around 6.30, the strange uneven beat of the German bombers' engines, the thuds and crack of the bombs and A.A. fire, the sudden glow of orange-red in the east or west or north or south, the bells of the fire engines and ambulances—everybody a bit tired and on edge.

Came 1941 and the start of the build-up of the great German armies in the East; Churchill warning Stalin, who, for some reason best known to himself, ignored not only our own but others from his own intelligence service. Was he, too, like the British Government in the 'thirties waiting for something to turn up?

May 1941, and the brilliant naval action in sinking the *Bismarck*. This was a triumph of intelligence co-ordination by the Naval Intelligence Department.

Crete was a disappointment intelligence-wise. We had been able to give General Freyburg a detailed account of the location, strength and timing of the German parachute drops several days in advance. Unfortunately the decision to evacuate the Island had already been taken, otherwise the parachute invasion might have been a nasty shock for Goering.

Came, also, the ding-dong battles in the Western Desert; Britain pouring out her last remaining cash to buy American destroyers and equipment; the Battle of the Atlantic.

The fateful 7th December, 1941, and the Japanese attack on Pearl Harbour which, I believe, history will argue might have been avoided if the Americans had been on their toes. Maybe this had something to do with the strong Anglophobia of General

MacArthur. He would not allow British officers to visit his head-quarters. I myself was refused permission and I know of one Air Commodore whom he had to receive and who, after the 'audience', was sent off to feed in the Sergeants' Mess.

Perhaps it was because MacArthur relied so much on Intelligence supplied by the British about Japanese ship movements that he resented British personnel. Maybe he was just sore about Pearl Harbour, and also the limelight that was given to the American forces in Europe.

I was up at Brisbane in Australia shortly after MacArthur had left on the first stage of his Pacific comeback on New Guinea. He had certainly done his best to propagate his own views about Britain amongst the Australian Air Force Command.

My reception was cool to say the least, and I quickly asked the Air Staff in Melbourne what cooked; MacArthur had brought relations between the Australian Air Staff in Melbourne and the Australian Air Command in Queensland near to crisis point.

I don't know how many of the traditionally lovely Brisbane girls finally became G.I. brides, but at the time of my visit I met a great many who were looking forward to becoming the wives of the inevitable big business tycoon who just happened to be temporarily a G.I. I hope they found out in time. I heard that the anti-British feelings aroused by MacArthur's propaganda were soon forgotten when the 'diggers' came home to find their girls bound for the U.S.A.

Brisbane is such an attractive, friendly town. I had known it first as a boy in the New Year of 1914, now at Xmas, 1944, thirty years later, its real people were just as friendly. I think Queensland is one of the most attractive parts of Australia.

October 1942, Alamein. Winston Churchill paid tribute in his history of the war to the fact that we managed to obtain the order of battle and plans of operations of Rommel's army now facing our own Eighth Army. Alamein was perhaps the turning point of the war. Churchill knew it, Montgomery knew it, and any criticism of the latter's use of the armour at his disposal must fade before the vital necessity to gain an overwhelming victory.

The knowledge of the whereabouts, strength and plan of attack of Rommel's forces must have helped Montgomery to carry out his own plan of holding Rommel's main attack in the south whilst 'hitting him for six' in the north. The orthodoxy of the German military thinking—if your enemy has one flank on the sea, attack him on his other flank and roll him back to the water—had worked in France in 1940 against the British; it had worked in 1942 in North Africa; but this time Montgomery was prepared for it.

The defeat of Rommel's desert army was turned into a rout and it was largely due to information supplied to Malta that the navy and air forces there were so brilliantly successful in sinking all and every one of the convoys of vital supplies for the retreating army which were shipped from Italy. I think I am correct in saying the only petrol Rommel got was some barrels which were washed ashore from a sunken supply vessel.

Whether it was the result of Rommel's defeat in Africa or maybe a general dissatisfaction with security inside Germany, Admiral Canaris, Hitler's Chief of Intelligence and Security, was in trouble.

In 1942 it was still possible to get in touch with enemy personnel through contacts in Lisbon or Madrid, but it was a little surprising when Canaris made an approach to his opposite number my own Chief. Unlike Hess's flying mission, which was a last attempt to get us to declare our neutrality and allow Hitler to get on with the job of eliminating Communism, Canaris proposed to stop hostilities by the elimination of Hitler and the Nazis.

We could, I think, have trusted the generals to restore the pre-war state of Western Europe, and even Poland, in exchange for our stopping the war in the West, though judging by the rather muddled failure of the generals to assassinate Hitler in July 1944, it seems doubtful whether Canaris and his friends could have carried it out any sooner or any better. It would certainly not have pleased Stalin, but why we should fall over backwards to appease those who were, and are, pledged to destroy our way of life I shall never understand.

In the event the contact with Canaris came to nothing. There is now little doubt that the Russian spy, Philby, had something to do with this.

Recovery

Autumn 1942, and the Americans came to Europe. It was at Norfolk House, the Combined Planning Headquarters for Operation 'Torch', that I first met both General Eisenhower and Mark Clark, so completely different from each other: Eisenhower, stocky, fair, blue-eyed, very calm and softly spoken, with an easy smile and built-in authority; Clark, tall, dark, impulsive, inclined to show off yet not quite sure of himself, I judged.

The combined British-American operation in North Africa was the outcome of much early disagreement between the American and British chiefs-of-staff. The former wanted to mount an invasion of Europe; Churchill insisted it was too risky at this stage of the war and our lack of adequate equipment. When North Africa was finally decided upon, the Americans insisted on landing far to the west, a mistake which was to cost us dear.

The Americans were a little naive about intelligence at this stage and would not believe our assurances that the Germans would never attempt to cut down through Spain to block the Straits of Gibraltar. They feared a second Crete on the Rock, but the physical difficulties of supply and reinforcement would have been too difficult.

In a way, it was comforting to know my old 'friend' Kesselring was the German commander in the Mediterranean; he had come a long way since our first meeting in 1934. I felt sure he would play it according to the book, both from lack of imagination and, also, because as an Air Force officer he could not risk the ridicule of the Army. He was convinced we were about to invade Sicily. Here was the orthodox German thinking: why land in North Africa and put the Mediterranean Sea between us and our final objective which must be Europe? Anyway, our landing in North Africa was unsuspected up to the last minute.

Not until a few days after the landing was I able to get to Algiers. Communication flights from Plymouth to Gibraltar by flying-boat were made available. The dusk take-off, the long flight out into the Atlantic to avoid enemy aircraft from France; then the south-easterly course to Gibraltar, dawn breaking over the Portuguese coast and as luck would have it, on arrival at Gibraltar, finding that the Air Officer Commanding was none other than 'Simmy' Simpson, who had been my first flight commander when

I joined No. 29 Fighter Squadron near Arras early in 1917. 'Simmy' was splendid; he had a nice house on the Rock and comfortable beds, but, what was much more important, was able to send me on to Algiers on an operational flight. At first, before connections were fully organised, one had to thumb a lift in whatever was going. It was dicey and maybe it took a week.

General Eisenhower had established his headquarters in the big white King George Hotel at Algiers. It looked out over the bay from a splendid position halfway up the hill behind the town and here were housed all the American staff, also Admiral Cunningham and his naval staff. It was Admiral Cunningham who, in fact, stole the show. Whether it was but a short journey from the hotel to his main headquarters afloat in the harbour, or whether it was farther afield, the Admiral was to be seen in his dark blue limousine, large Union Jack fluttering proudly from the bows, his immaculate white and gold uniform bright in the sunshine and, indeed, gleaming at night when the interior of the car was well and fully lit up. The leisurely procession of this illuminated limousine was almost regal and the Algerians certainly thought he was the top boy.

As it can be imagined, Algiers in 1942 was a wonderful change from the November skies of London. The gardens of the whitewashed villas were full of plumbago and oleander and great drifts of purple bougainvillaea dazzling in the North African sun; oranges, too, perhaps too many of them.

But this was not what I was there for. Despite frantic efforts by General Anderson and Air Marshal Welsh to make good the mistake of the too far western landings and to push eastward as quickly as possible, Kesselring reacted with remarkable speed to repair his own mistake. There was a very rapid build-up of German ground and air forces at Tunis and Bizerta where the Germans had the full advantage of proper aerodromes.

Shortly after I arrived a ship came in from America carrying a flock of fully-fledged colonels. The eagles on their shoulders all looked a bit fresh from the nest and, on enquiry, I found they were, in fact, vice-presidents of various business firms in the United States who had come to follow up conquest with trade. About the same time a boatload of jeeps was unloaded and parked a mile or two outside the town. If it was intended to introduce the Arab to the jeep it was certainly successful—two days later not a jeep was to be found!

As a result of the influx of colonels, the hotel became rather crowded. In any case, I had to see the British Air and Army commanders; but where to find them? They were no longer in Algiers. Eventually I ran Air Marshal Freddie Welsh to ground not far from Maison Blanche Aerodrome, and when I asked him why he had gone so far away from the Eisenhower headquarters he said, to put it politely, that he felt there was, in these initial stages, too much confusion at General Headquarters to allow for constructive thinking and the conduct of the urgent air operations that were required.

General Anderson was in command of the British 1st Army in North Africa. He was a Scot, and some miles east of Algiers there were some hills which reminded him of Scotland; also they were well nigh inaccessible. He, too, liked to be on his own. I eventually found him and spent a very pleasant weekend discussing amongst other things secondary education in Scotland, which was his pet subject. While I was there an incident occurred which took my thoughts straight back to Germany.

On a quiet Sunday morning there arose a terrific racket of large cars coming down the lane to the lonely farmhouse which was Anderson's headquarters. Two vast black Cadillacs approached as fast as the narrow road allowed; the dust rose in a cloud; out of the first, as it drew up, brakes protesting, jumped half a dozen black-booted khaki-clad bodyguards, hands-on-holster types. Out of the second, tall and elegant, long black boots gleaming in the sun, black eye-brows drawn down, sprang—no, not Hess, but— Mark Clark. He, too, had found Anderson's hideout.

Nevertheless, General Mark Clark was a very courageous man. It was he who had gone secretly to France and arranged the escape, by British submarine, of General Giraud to Algeria. It was vital to have some prominent French general with the Allied forces to rally the French Algerians to our cause.

Admiral Darlan, who was already in Algiers, was a doubtful starter; in fact, he explained to one of my French colleagues that he was fearful for his pension if he openly joined the Allies in defiance of the Vichy Government. He need not have worried; he was murdered in his 'Palace' shortly afterwards.

General Anderson explained why he liked being in this remote spot—it was close above the single-line railway which had to take all the supplies up from Algiers to where our troops were then fighting, and he liked to keep a personal eye on the trains and see that they went by regularly. But I am quite sure the bracken and the silver birch had a great deal to do with it.

It was this lack of close liaison between the various commanders and staff on this first Anglo-American operation which prompted the very strict rules for co-operation in Operation Overlord, the great adventure into Europe.

Perhaps one of my greatest joys was to get a phone message one morning at the King George Hotel from Georges Ronin. He and a number of his colleagues had managed to board a plane to Algiers after they had evaded the German occupation of Southern France which Hitler had ordered after our landings in Algeria. Georges, too, was pleased to be out of the precarious position he had held in Vichy for the past two years. Now at last he felt he could really help again. He did. He already had his pre-war contacts in Tunis where it was vital we should know of the German army and air build up.

It was, too, a splendid lunch they gave me on the sun-drenched roof-top of the little white villa above the deep blue bay of Algiers.

The Americans were quick to adopt our technique of high altitude spy photography as soon as they got going in North Africa. Roosevelt's son was given command of their unit which produced miles of film. The total amount of photographs taken by the Allies from the air was truly prodigious and it paid off. Curiously, the Germans never got beyond their pre-war technique.

On a later visit to Algiers I had to go up east to Constantine, across the Setif Plain which, I was told, once supplied most of the grain for Rome. Now this wonderful stretch of country appeared almost deserted. A few indolent Arabs in their unwashed shifts strolled about the villages, as always the young men holding hands. I wonder if the Romans succeeded in making them work. At Constantine I met, for the first time, General Spaatz who was commanding the American Air Forces; he was finding his feet very quickly. I came to know him better as the war went on and I have always had a warm spot for this cheerful guitar-playing airman.

Our own front-lines were well up in Tunisia by this time but there was still plenty of resistance. I had some difficulty in re-assuring George Lawson, who was commanding the Royal Air Force up front, that the German fighter aircraft strength was not, in fact, three times his own. The trouble was the Germans were able to operate their fighters from proper aerodromes whilst poor Lawson had a job to find a flat piece of ground that was not a bog.

Getting a lift back from Algeria to Gibraltar and then back to England was not as easy as the other way; in 1942 it was a question of thumbing a lift. The bar at the Rock Hotel on Gibraltar was ever full of 'lift-thumbers'. On one occasion when I was bringing Georges Ronin back to London for a visit, Simpson got us a lift on a Catalina flying-boat which was on delivery flight from the U.S.A. These remarkable boats could fly over three thousand miles non-stop—a considerable achievement in 1942—and after a leisurely over-night trip from Gibraltar we arrived off the English coast at dawn. Sometimes I can still smell the sausages and baked beans that we fried in the little blacked-out cabin about midnight.

Alas, we found England blanketed in cotton-wool fog. It was a dreary business trying to get permission to land. We tried the whole coast of England, right up the west to Scotland, down the East Coast and round again to Plymouth. No dice. Everything and everywhere was absolutely fogbound so we were advised to go all the way back to Gibraltar. Though possible, this did not seem a good idea, so, after a chat with the pilot, we went right down on the sea which was as calm as a mill-pond under the fog. He made an excellent landing and, once we were down, we told Plymouth that we were now a boat and were coming in on the water. Fortunately they had a radio beam from their station at Mount Batten which guided us through the harbour mouth. I have always liked flying-boats.

Another time General Spaatz gave me a lift in his personal aircraft which did a weekly round trip to London and, amongst other things, refuelled at Fortnum and Mason's! It so happened that War Minister Grigg was my fellow passenger. The Flying-Fortress was a well-armed machine and the pilots did not believe in going very far out into the Atlantic in order to miss the German fighters from the French coast. I am glad to say the one who came and had a look at us sheered off after a few bursts from the Fortress's gunners. Grigg seemed very bored and pre-occupied with the flight. I offered him a detective story to take his mind off things, but he replied that he was afraid my sort of reading was not in his line at all.

Just as the Germans were finally driven out of North Africa I went to Tunis. In a lovely villa high up on the hills overlooking the blue bay lived a very gracious Englishwoman, the mother of my very good friend who first introduced me to Barnes Wallis in England. I had much to tell her about London and her son. She now lived in a small part of the villa and had done so throughout the war; the rest of the house had been occupied by the German Air Force; but now it was the gentle twang of General Spaatz's guitar which echoed along the cloisters of this paradise. My hostess most kindly put me up for the night and gave me a superb meal. The delicious sea-food came from the bay below, the heavy scent from the jasmine outside the window.

She told me of the amusing evacuation of Tunis by the Germans. German troops were still strolling about the streets of the town below when the first English tanks rumbled in. The German Air Force Staff panicked completely. They ran out of the house and down the steep, shrub-covered hill to the water below, hoping to get away by some sort of boat. Few did, and of course there was much to clear up in the house before the Americans could occupy it; much of interest, too.

Round the coast, close to Carthage, the water was warm and London a long way off. General Alexander was showing me his caravan site near his tented headquarters. He told me that during the whole of the desert campaign he always chose a site for his caravan that gave him a view of either the sunset or the sunrise over the desert, and here, in Tunisia, where there were trees to add to the scene, he had certainly found a lovely spot. Kesselring and his troops were well and truly over the other side of the sea in Sicily, but they could still try to retaliate for the Taormina affair. In consequence the headquarters was carefully camouflaged amongst the pine trees. Earl Alexander was one of those people who made you feel the job you were doing was really worth while —a rare gift.

The Royal Air Force Headquarters were not far away and I had to see Tedder in the afternoon. I had known him for a very long time and it was my privilege to visit this truly delightful person at the various S.H.A.E.F headquarters many times during the war. Never did I see him ruffled, seldom without his pipe.

After the fall of Tunis I had to go on to Cairo. Admiral Ramsay, who had been up in Algeria for a conference on the coming invasion of Sicily, gave me a lift back to Cairo in his aircraft. After the black-outs and cold of England it was absolute heaven. I had many old friends there, but the first thing to do was to have a swim at the Gezira Club pool; then lunch in town with Tom Mappelbeck, who had been a prisoner-of-war with me, and whose young brother, John, was now one of my staff in North Africa. Tom had a lovely flat looking out over the Nile. Just to feel the real warmth of Egypt and to see everyone in gay summer clothing was a tonic; dinner out of doors at the Club under the stars, fairy lights strung between the graceful palms, good food, soft-footed waiters; the sound of music and the gay girls—it was rather hard to leave, was Cairo in 1943.

The brilliant planning by Admiral Ramsay for the invasion of Sicily was the forerunner of his success in the great operation overland. Not only had it been possible to give the planners the most detailed photographs of the invasion beaches but it had also been possible to give them the strength and locations of the enemy units on the island, and even more important, the fact that Kesselring had no notion that the operation would be against Sicily.

Surprise was also achieved at Anzio beach in Italy and only the failure of Mark Clark to follow it up turned it into a very bloody stalemate.

Winston Churchill had been out to see Alexander when progress against Kesselring's defence of the Monte Cassino line was at a standstill. Shortly after he returned I was summoned round to his war room late one Sunday night. He asked me if there was any news from Cassino. I, of course, was unaware of the plan to send the French Moroccan troops over the mountains to outflank the enemy lines, and there had been no squeal out of Kesselring. Churchill seemed disappointed but by next morning we were able to give him news of the enemy's discomfiture.

It was our ability to inform Alexander and Mark Clark of Kesselring's decision to retreat to the north of Rome which gave the latter his chance to 'change the plans' of his C.-in-C. Alexander and make the dramatic American entry into Rome with Mark Clark in the van. It was, I think, in character.

19

Operation Overlord: Liberation

I suppose for all those who took part in it, the final stages of the preparation for 'D-Day' and the fateful days of its delay due to the exceptionally bad June weather were the most nerve-wracking of the whole war. For the three weeks before the kick-off I never left the office day or night except to go down to the country house near Portsmouth which was the Headquarters of the Supreme Commander. If there had been any indication from any of our sources in France or Belgium that Army or Air reinforcements were being sent to the true invasion area, especially troops from the Calais area southward, or any parts of the main reserve of armoured units around Paris in the direction of the coast, then our plans might have had to be modified.

How different the story now to those dark days of September 1940 when The Few were fighting for our lives in the air, and the troops and aircraft and invasion barges for Hitler's Operation Sea Lion were piling up across the Channel.

The German Air Force had never developed our technique of high-altitude photography, and we saw to it that no German spotter planes got near enough to our own creeks and harbours along the South Coast to estimate with sufficient accuracy our build-up or its destination. There was almost complete wireless silence except for the signals of Patton's phoney army in Kent. Nevertheless, when one thinks of the thousands of people concerned in this vast operation, it was a tribute to the superb security consciousness of everybody that nothing did, in fact, get out.

Our own security department did a magnificent job in pinpointing the few German Agents who had been planted in Britain with wireless sets to give warnings to the Germans of invasion plans. Some of these were co-operative and their flow of traffic back to Germany was 'maintained' in order not to arouse suspicion by a complete blackout; others, not so co-operative, were found more secluded quarters.

The threat of the V-1 secret weapon, the doodle-bug, was now imminent and it looked like a race against time as to whether Overlord would be able to liberate the French Coast before a flood of destruction descended on London, and other vital centres.

One of the Germans' most experienced agents was 'introduced' into England to pinpoint the important Allied Headquarters and supply bases for Overlord and in due course to report on the results of the V-1 attacks. He was duly 'picked up' and by the time the V-1 attacks started a week after D-Day the inaccuracy of the pinpoints which were sent back to the Germans spared the several harmless country houses near the South Coast which were supposed to accommodate our illustrious Commanders and their staffs.

As I said earlier in this book, it is people who have always interested me—their characters and reactions and the effects these have had on our own lives—for there is surely no doubt nowadays in men's minds that despite the democracies it is the individual, whether he be dictator, president, or prime minister, who really shapes the pattern of our lives.

Here I am concerned only with the few men whom I knew and worked with, who, in World War Two, held our future in their hands. Of Winston Churchill I have confined my remarks to a few short anecdotes; his history now belongs to everyone. When with him, either alone or with others, I never experienced the quick reply or hasty judgement. Always one could feel the problem being turned this way and that in his mind, albeit remarkably quickly, before the decision was taken. The command was ever polite whatever the rank of the recipient and often in language that one would have taken a long time to compose oneself.

Lord Tedder, with whom I had worked in the Air Ministry in the 'thirties, and who had helped to get the Spitfires for the Photographic Unit against the pressures of Fighter Command,

I had once seen almost excited when chance had put him on the road to fame.

It was back in 1941 and I had just come into the Royal Air Force Club for lunch. I used to walk back from Whitehall across St. James's Park—the flowers were always a tonic. Coming down the hall of the Club at something above normal flying speed was Air Marshal Tedder, as he then was. I remarked that he seemed in a bit of a hurry. He grinned, took the pipe out of his mouth, and gave me the news. 'Poor old Boyd has made a forced landing in Italy on his way to take up command of the Middle East. Fred, isn't it a bit of luck!' he said. 'Have to fly out this afternoon. See you sometime.'

One often hears how luck has played a part in the careers of the great. Maybe it does, but unless the men play their luck the right way and have the combination of a number-one brain, a number-one ambition, tough health *and* charm, they do not often make the grade.

Tedder first met Eisenhower at the Casablanca Conference and they 'clicked' straight away. Tedder told me how it came about; they had started talking about the role of the Air Force in the war of movement. There were some divergent views on this subject at the time, but the close air support of the army which Tedder believed in and had practised in the Western Desert fitted in with Eisenhower's views so precisely that they found themselves in complete agreement. When the North African campaign had been tidied up, Tedder became Eisenhower's Deputy Supreme Commander for the great operation into Europe.

He was one of the most unflappable men I have known, and by that I mean unflappable deep within himself. I have seen many people in a crisis assume a rigid pose of outward calm, either by will-power or training, but it is the person whose calm is natural whose judgement remains unimpaired. I don't believe Tedder's pipe gave off any accelerated smoke signals at the most crucial moments of Operation Overlord than it did on a calm day in his office as Chief of Air Staff. He did admit to me when I went down to S.H.A.E.F. Headquarters near Portsmouth on June 4th, 1944, that the strain of the D-Day postponements was increasing his tobacco bill, but I could detect no increase in the speed of puff.

Montgomery as a person I knew little. Even after our most valuable and reliable source of intelligence had supplied him with Rommel's vital order of battle before Alamein, Montgomery did not care to admit the existence of any outside intelligence. He was the only commander who disliked my visiting his Head-quarters. Fortunately I was allowed to confer with Bill Williams, his Chief Intelligence Officer, who more than made up for the lack of welcome elsewhere. But the story of Montgomery in Operation Overlord weaves in so closely with that of United States' Generals Omar Bradley and Patton, and even with his Commander-in-Chief, Eisenhower, that in brief I will give an outline of his relations with these men as seen purely from the point of view of an Intelligence officer.

Omar Bradley was a quiet, tall man with smiling eyes under straight dark eyebrows; deep lines ran to a wide mouth which grew even wider when he smiled with that, too.

When I met him in London during the planning stage of Overlord he seemed to me a little too diffident, a bit worried and not yet sure of himself. He was so completely opposite in manner to the shorter, confident, rather staccato-voiced victor of Alamein, and seemed on the defensive. Eisenhower obviously could not show him too much patronage. Montgomery was inevitably involved with General Bradley; yet I somehow sensed that Bradley and Montgomery did not really hit it off.

Perhaps it was because of his feeling that he must justify him-self as Commander of the American First Army, who had been given the toughest landing beach on the Normandy coast, that he failed to accept the offer by Montgomery of the special armoured vehicles designed to storm the beach-heads. He also failed to accept the intelligence report that an additional new German Division had moved into position opposite his Omaha beach.

The results were grim. The story of Omaha beach is well known and it was a somewhat chastened Bradley whom I went to see at his first field headquarters a few days after the landing. I had to convince him that if important strategical information was given to him it would have been checked and could be accepted. He was very friendly, and anxious that I should keep in closest touch with his Chief Intelligence Officer. We became great friends and remained so throughout the rest of the war.

The mobile headquarters of the American Armies and Air Forces were truly magnificent—enormous caravans, with all 'mod-cons', and usually a very comfortable one for visitors. General Bradley's first headquarters site in Normandy was only a mile or two inland and was actually in range of German guns, but it was well camouflaged and the caravans were spread around the northern edge of a wood in a semi-circle, making a sort of village green in the middle. As usual, the feeding arrangements were superb.

It was at last a warm summer morning in that early half of June, 1944. I was leaning on the half-door of my caravan and looking forward to a good breakfast when there was a sudden commotion on the village green; staff officers hurrying hither and thither, Bradley himself obviously giving orders which were being transmitted at the double. I was alarmed. I knew his army was having trouble trying to break out to St. Lo in the south. Had there been a sudden reverse? Should we have to evacuate?

I sought out my Intelligence contact; he told me the news. Montgomery was coming over to visit Bradley. Montgomery was commanding both his own and Bradley's armies during the initial operations. This was their first personal meeting since before D-Day and I sensed that Bradley was not going to enjoy it.

And as if this wasn't enough for an already worried commander, who should decide to drop in but General Patton, complete with his well-known white bull terrier. He must have been kept well out of sight until after Monty had left, but around midday I saw this familiar figure strolling around the camp. Now, General Patton was still supposed to be commanding a great American invasion force in Kent. Actually, there was no such force, but so long as Patton was plainly visible in Kent and his fictitious units kept calling each other up on their radios, the Germans kept a large part of their anti-invasion forces up around Calais because they were convinced that this was where the main attack would come. If they had known that Patton's Army in Kent was but a myth they would have made our progress from the Normandy beaches very much more difficult. That this unpredictable General Patton should have left his phantom army at this critical stage was unthinkable. What to do?

The headquarters was full of war correspondents and if they let out any breath of Patton's presence there would be trouble. Patton just could not keep away from a battle. The war correspondents were summoned at once by my very good friend, the Chief Intelligence Officer on General Bradley's staff, who took me along to this odd press conference which went something like this:

'Gentlemen. Some of you may have inadvertently seen what you might have taken to be General Patton at these headquarters. Well, you haven't. No questions. Good morning.' After that the General concerned felt himself free to stroll around with his faithful dog and feel once again that he was fighting someone.

I had met General Patton when he first arrived in Algeria. He was not wearing either his gold-plaited steel helmet or his six revolvers when I saw him. He was a very delightful person who, when I talked to him about 'intelligence', said very nicely: 'You know, you'd better talk to my staff officers about this. I don't know much about these things. I just like fighting.' And he did.

General Bradley promised me he would take full notice of our intelligence in future. He did!

The orthodox military thinking of Rundstedt, Commander-in-Chief West, backed up by Hitler who was himself deeply immersed in his Eastern Campaign far away in East Prussia, failed to support the view of Rommel, in command of the French coast, that all available German forces should be used at once in an attempt to throw the Allies off their slender foothold in Normandy back into the sea.

By the end of June it was too late and the younger generals, including Rommel, saw the beginning of the end. In a last desperate revolt the disgruntled generals made their final attempt to assassinate Hitler at his Eastern Headquarters on July 20th. Had they succeeded, no doubt they would have asked for an armistice and, as in 1918, tried to salvage something out of the wreck.

Operation Overlord: Liberation

By the end of July the Americans, under Bradley, after a magnificent effort, had reached the base of the Cherbourg peninsula, where the ancient town of Avranches sits proudly and comfortably on the top of its big round hill commanding the roads and surveying the country for many miles around.

The attempt on his life, the involvement of the illustrious Rommel, and the American advance seem finally to have woken Hitler up to the necessity to do something in the West.

And now, at this critical moment, came another of those reports from our most valuable and reliable intelligence service. Hitler, in his own, now undisputed, opinion the great master of strategy, issued orders that Von Kluge, who commanded the German armies in Normandy, was to use the whole of the great strategic reserve of armoured units which was stationed close to Paris, and included the famous tank units of the S.S. Panzer Corps, in one great drive westwards to Avranches, when it would split the Allied invasion armies in two and roll the two halves back into the sea. So this was it. It is doubtful if the more orthodox generals would have risked such a move.

Bradley now acted with great speed, and started Patton's Third Army on its famous break-out to the East, with orders to turn north behind Von Kluge's forces.

Suppressed excitement at Allied Headquarters was intense as, gradually, sightings of the vast tank armada were made on its journey westward. Montgomery's task was to push southward from Caen, meet up with the Americans, and so close the ring around the now famous Falaise Trap. There was little doubt in everyone's mind that this would be the turning point in the second battle of France.

Von Kluge's westward attack was duly held before Avranches and the pincers started to close around him. By mid-August the eastern exit from the trap was almost closed but whilst the Americans had by this time come northwards right up to the British Sector boundary, Montgomery's forces had failed to come far enough south to meet them.

Bradley waited a vital twenty-four hours for an invitation from Montgomery to cross the British Sector boundary and finish off the gap but it did not come. Bradley was not amused.

By this time the trapped German troops were streaming eastwards through the gap, so Bradley sent two corps forward to try to trap them again on the Seine. By the time Montgomery finally closed the gap several days later many of the crack troops of the S.S. Panzer Corps had escaped, as Montgomery was to find to his cost later at Arnhem.

So much is history. Bradley had kept his promise to take our intelligence seriously. Falaise was the turning point in the west.

It was at this time that I sensed a great change in General Bradley. Gone was the diffidence, and the sense of being only a second-in-command to the redoubtable Montgomery. There was a new ring of quiet but determined authority in his voice and in his bearing. He knew what he was doing and he was doing it well. He was now free of Montgomery's command and ranked equal with him under Eisenhower. The dramatic race across France by Patton's Third Army was perhaps one of the most thrilling episodes of the war. He certainly got the headlines both in Britain and in America. When he was heading eastwards at speed, he was even more difficult to find than Anderson had been in Algeria.

I eventually got news that he was going to set up a temporary headquarters for a day or two in a little wood not far from Verdun, so I decided to go and wait until he arrived. As it happened, his tanks had just captured a whole train-load of champagne, mostly Veuve Cliquot, which the Germans had failed to get away in time. Oh boy, what an evening! The usual procedure for setting up camp was for a couple of bulldozers to open up some roads and clearings in a selected wood; then in would come the caravans and the food. This particular night the bulldozers had enjoyed themselves. The crazy clearings that they had made were more like the Hampton Court Maze, and the long caravans could not negotiate the erratic curves! So there were tents, and champagne. No time to open the bottles—just knock the heads off!

The tanks had made such rapid progress that, at times, they were in danger of running out of fuel, and on this particular evening they were getting a bit short. All their fuel had first to come across the Channel and then try to catch up with them. In their haste to escape, the Germans had also left behind a certain amount of petrol which had at once been absorbed by the local inhabitants.

Patton's tanks bartered champagne for petrol, bottle for bottle; this must really have pleased the logical Frenchmen.

There were many stories about General Patton and his toughness with his men, but I never met one who did not worship him. He certainly taught the Germans something about *blitzkriegs* in the second battle of France.

As our armies pushed eastward the question of bringing up supplies became paramount. There was a special route kept clear for transport called the Red Ball Route, which eventually ran from Cherbourg right up to the Rhine. It was a marvel of transport organisation and the toughness of the American Negro drivers who kept their trucks running at high speed night and day in all weathers was quite amazing. It was quite unlike the first arrival of those same drivers in England in 1943.

I was on my way to Southampton one day when I met a long convoy of newly arrived American trucks drawn up on the wrong side of the road. The Negro drivers were lying, apparently asleep, on the grassy bank beside the road. I stopped to ask the smart Negro sergeant how they were getting on and how they liked coming over here.

With a liquid Southern drawl he replied: 'Yes, sah, we jus' arrived.'

'Are your men very tired?' I asked.

'Oh, no, sah, they're jus' restin' in case they might get tired, sah.'

I often thought of this incident when I saw the convoys belting along the Red Ball Route on a stormy night. There were just the odd ones who found the strain too much and, one day soon after the liberation of Paris, I went up to the Eiffel Tower to look at the flat where I had spent so many happy times before the war, and there, at the Champ de Mars, was the greatest, if not the original, black market. Sometimes a whole truck-load of food, plus the truck, would change hands and the driver would find rest and solace with no colour-bar.

Paris, short of food and petrol, everybody riding on bicycles reminding me of Holland before the war, was not the same without Georges Ronin. He had not come back from Algiers, wisely, because the Maquis were running a bit wild, and anyone suspected of collaboration with the Nazis or with Vichy was being rounded up and often quietly disposed of. It was not until after the war, when the Gaullists wanted to put him on trial, that I told General de Gaulle the truth. I had not dared to do so before. Georges Ronin returned to France with full rank and honour. He died in 1956, a very gallant Frenchman.

Cheese has always been one of my favourite foods. The sight of pile upon pile of unboxed Camembert cheese in Normandy soon after D-Day shocked me. I bought some butter from a farmer's wife and chatted with her while her daughter weighed it up—real butter, all ten pounds of it, in 1944. The old woman was glad to sell it. Yes, they had been forced to make so many cheeses for the Germans to send back to their own country, but of course they had taken the cream off first and made the cheeses out of the skim; this, then, was the answer to the piles of useless cheeses that dotted the roadsides. She told me that the German soldiers had been only too willing to buy the butter; it had been very good business but now things would be different She supposed the best side had won but she would not be able to sell her cheeses, as well as butter, any more. Did she want to be liberated, I asked. Well, would we pay her as well as the Germans had done? The French 'peasants' are logical!

The tragedy of Arnhem always puzzled me. Patton had continued his spectacular advance towards the German frontier. Montgomery had done equally well up the west coast through Belgium, with Bradley further inland, but now, as the British armies approached Holland with all its rivers and waterways across its path, Montgomery wanted to try a rapid airborne thrust up into Holland. The total advance had been so rapid, and with the Channel ports still held by German garrisons Eisenhower wanted to consolidate and organise his supply routes for the final assault on Germany.

Montgomery's unwillingness to accept this policy all but cost him his job. Winston Churchill saved him, and Eisenhower reluctantly agreed to allow him to go ahead with his airborne project, despite the protests of that other tall, quiet, but very efficient British General Dempsey commanding the British 2nd

Army. Bradley called it 'a sixty mile salient to be driven up a side alley.' It was designed to secure the main bridges over the great waterways of Holland.

For some time our sources in Holland had been reporting that the Dutch Resistance had been badly penetrated by the Nazis, and many were the gallant Dutchmen who were found out and executed. It was not surprising, therefore, that when the special wartime organisation in England, which helped the Resistance movements in Europe, dropped large amounts of arms into Holland in order to give the Resistance some teeth with which to help the coming operation, not only did most of them fall into Nazi hands but the Germans were alerted that something was brewing. I was advised at the time that a Dutch Nazi who had somehow insinuated himself into the London end of the Resistance helpers defected to Holland shortly before the airborne operation. The matter was dealt with at a very exalted level and was a great blow to all those loyal Dutchmen who did so much to help regain their country's liberty. From the manner in which the Germans reacted at Arnhem it seems evident that the operation was betrayed.

Montgomery believed that there would be no organised resistance and that the German forces were in a state of dis-organisation. Dutch Resistance Intelligence, however, reported that parts of the two crack S.S. Panzer Division troops that had escaped from Falaise were in the area.

Anyway, the operation was proceeded with. An Intelligence Officer is by the nature of his work apt to attach too much importance to 'information' and maybe not enough to the military and political considerations involved. In the event the Germans had scraped together enough troops around the core of their almost fanatical S.S. Panzer Divisions to break the airborne attack on Arnhem with such tragic results.

The German Staff's ability to reorganise their forces into some sort of effective fighting units was to be shown again when they were able to mount their last surprise offensive from the Ardennes towards Brussels. It was once again a repetition of their last desperate offensive in France in 1918 and it drove deep into the Allied Front, dividing Bradley's army. The speed with which Patton came to the rescue and sealed off any hope of a German breakout southward astonished everyone, but Bradley's cup was not yet full. At Montgomery's suggestion the northern half of Bradley's army, now divided from the southern half by the German thrust, was once again put under Montgomery. Two days passed before the British Commander moved to stop the thrust,

The next time I saw him Bradley's eyes were smiling as usual but his jaw had a rather harder line. The offensive had been halted and the enemy driven back to his own Fatherland. Bradley's headquarters were now in a hotel in Luxembourg. The Allies were at the throat of the Germans now and the Ruhr lay ahead. Once that had fallen it was the end of Hitler's armies in the west.

I had come down from Brussels, which had known little of this war, by way of Trier, where I had been a prisoner-of-war in the First World War; the years between had not changed the sleepy old town very much. I had given General Bradley all the help I could ever since I had known him, and now, in his hotel-room office which was small and warm, I gave him all the information I could about his opposition. I had tremendous admiration for this quiet general. I had seen him grow so rapidly in stature through bad times and good, and now he was unmistakably a tried and authoritative commander.

He thanked me warmly for the information, asked me to wait and then summoned his whole staff. He then gave the simple but concise orders for the advance into the Ruhr, and Germany.

Turning to me, with a twinkle in his eye he said: 'Now I think we could all do with a bite of food.' We could.

I made so many good friends amongst the American forces and had such splendid meals in their well found messes, it was not surprising I used to extend my visits to France whenever possible; whether it was with General Simpson, that tall, rather quiet commander of the Ninth Army, or with my old friends at General Bradley's headquarters, where the General himself always made me welcome; or young Air General Quesada and the gay evenings with his Air Force lads, or at Patton's ever-moving caravanserai, where all was speed and hurry and 'how are you?' and 'goodbye till next time'. And back in England the ever-friendly Carl Spaatz and the redoubtable General Doolittle. They were a marvellous lot of men and one of my most treasured possessions is the Order of Merit they gave me at the end of the war.

World War Two will, I think be remembered by historians of the future not only for its great sea, land and air battles but also for its 'Intelligence' on the grand scale.

We read of the great German Master Spy, General Reinhard Gehlen, whose agents in the Russian hierarchy kept the German General Staff informed of every move in the Russian strategy, and of the small group of anti-Nazi German officers who, in turn, kept the Russian General Staff informed of the strategical moves of the German armies in the East.

It is perhaps comforting to know that the empty corner of the square was the one where the German General Staff never knew what the Western Allies were going to do next until after the event.

20

Conclusion

The final attempt by the Army to assassinate Hitler had been made in July of 1944. It failed. It was the natural outcome of the long struggle between Hitler and the generals but now, at last, Hitler put an end once and for all to the old political power of the soldiers.

Ever since the time when the invasion of England had been abandoned Hitler had taken more and more of the direction of the war into his own hands, and there is little doubt that his personal orders to the German forces in France at the time of our landings contributed to our own successes. It was inevitable, therefore, that as soon as the point was reached when the generals realised they could no longer win, or even draw, the war, they should try to get rid of Hitler and once again, as in 1918, try and get a patched-up armistice which would leave them some shreds to which they could cling and, in due course, revive their old power. But Hitler had other ideas. Never, never, would he ask for peace. He envisaged either a Thousand-Year Reich or nothing, and if it was nothing he would take as many people into the pit with him as he could, to a flourish of Wagnerian trumpets.

For this demented Dictator, his gods had done their work in traditional sequence. The last days of Rosenberg, too, are public property. We know that he was tried with his fellow-Nazis at Nuremberg and was hanged, but the history of his activities during the war is a little obscure.

My own guess is that the Nordic nonsense was of very little use once the war had really begun, and that after the Americans had come in there was little outside diplomacy that Rosenberg could try his hand at. I expect they all wondered what they could do with him; after all, he had been one of the original and close personal friends of Hitler. After the flight to England of his other close friend, Hess, and the advent of the intriguing Bormann into Hitler's circle, I have no doubt that the Bormann 'fans' wanted to get Rosenberg as far away from Hitler as they could.

The triumvirate was broken up—it was never popular with the more aspiring Nazis, anyway—so why not push Rosenberg out somewhere onto the Eastern Front? After all, he had 'played' with the Ukrainians before the war and it was certainly necessary to get him fully implicated with the rest of them in the Jewish slaughter so that he could not escape the collective guilt should the occasion ever arise.

I think that is probably why Rosenberg was sent as Governor of the occupied Ukraine where so many of the terrible atrocities took place. But I still believe he was used as a puppet; I cannot see him in the role of a killer. I think that by this time Hitler himself was so involved with the Army that the black German S.S. had taken over the whole ghastly business and that very few people, excepting Himmler and his vile henchmen, had much say in it.

No doubt dictators will continue to spring up if they think they have got the answer, but what a bunch of amateurs the Nazis really were when it came to dealing with the big world outside Germany.

One mistake, however, Hitler did not make and that was to under-estimate the importance of keeping Britain neutral. He had the utmost respect for the British people, and he knew from World War One that the 'British Bulldog' was no caricature. Hitler used every means and everybody he could to persuade us to keep out of World War Two. How right he was. Were we? I have touched on this point earlier in this book, and I believe that we missed the greatest opportunity in our history. Perhaps we lacked the statesmen in the 1930s who could see over the horizon.

Now, as I look back over the past thirty years, I allow myself perchance to dream of a world in which the two major forces for evil in modern times, the Nazis and the Communists, had been allowed to fight each other to a standstill of destruction; of a strong and powerful Britain able to play her role in the translation of the *Pax Atlantica* into the *Pax Orbi*. What a wonderful job it would have been for the young of Britain to deal with all manner of men and nations, with all our years of experience to back them up.

What a chance to have been able to hand over to self-government, gradually and peacefully, the African tribal states of our Colonial Empire, instead of being rushed into premature disintegration by so-called political leaders inflamed with lust for power and hatred whipped up by the Communists, and resulting in disruption, massacre, and all the horrors of the old tribal wars.

What a chance for a Britain not ruined by a Second World War, but prosperous enough to have taken a great leap forward in social justice, unbedevilled by the play of insidious propaganda on ignorance and mistrust. What a chance to have planned her towns and cities, roads and industries, to give everyone more light and happiness and not have to 'penny pinch' all the time.

What a chance for a Britain, powerful enough to have made her voice heard and, in the deep background, the nuclear power to deter the upsurge of any new dictator.

And in the event, in February 1945, the ailing Roosevelt, the man who had championed the British and brought a great American army to Europe, ignoring the warning voice of Churchill at the Yalta Conference, believed he was a match for the wily Stalin in a game of chess with the countries of Eastern Europe as the pawns. Stalin won, and came a step nearer to his real objective —the capture of the kings and queens and knights and castles of Western Europe.

It may be true that the Chinese are willing to wait centuries for their final overthrow of the 'pink skinned' races, but the Russians are not so patient in their determination to have one communist world directed from Moscow. Stalin at that time knew nothing of the atom bomb, otherwise he would not have gone straight home and started to plan the military take-over of all Western Europe as well as the East, which he had now won. How nearly the Russians did not stop when they met up with the Allies in Germany is well known; but if their bluff was called and the gamble did not come off in 1945, it was destined to do so ten years later when the dust had settled. And then came the blow to Stalin's dreams, the atom bomb. This changed the whole picture. No longer could the Communists use military conquest to force their doctrines on the Western Democracies; now they themselves were in dire danger if they went too far or too fast.

We shall never know just how much Russian gold it took to bend the souls of a number of supreme traitors who, in the name of international science, sold the nuclear secrets to Moscow. Despite the nuclear bomb, the number one objective of world communism has never been abandoned.

Not until the Russians realised, after World War Two, that military conquest was out did they start to build up one of the most powerful and insidious psychological warfare and propaganda machines the world has known. In the words of Krushchev, the Communists would 'bury' us, presumably under the rubble of an economy which they hoped would be brought tottering to the ground. How busy they were doing everything in their power to force the premature break-up of the Colonial Empire; fomenting industrial unrest by rubbing salt into every little sore that could produce a strike or the disruption of our production and exports; infiltrating into any organisation, such as the Campaign for Nuclear Disarmament by Britain, which might serve their purpose. Using the full force of their propaganda machine to try to drive a wedge between Britain and their arch enemy, America; America that had baulked them in Korea, and was trying to save the whole of South-East Asia from their tyranny by stopping their aggression in Vietnam.

Trying to undermine public confidence in public men by use of sex and so-called satire and encouraging, with trained agitators, the abandonment of self-discipline amongst an un-washed, amoral minority of ignorant youngsters. It is time to take stock and find just how deeply the Communist virus has pene-trated into this country, and whether we are not already inviting with a permissive society a takeover bid by the gentlemen with a long red tail. Is it, perhaps, that the worst aspects of our society are given too much publicity, or am I on the wrong soap box? A rather battered 'Life-Buoy' vintage!

The hard-core Communists in Britain know quite well that they are unlikely to be able to seize power in this country through the ballot box. Their only real chance to set up their odious type of dictatorship is by reducing this country to chaos, economically and morally. Hunger and unemployment breed riots and blood-shed. Who knows whether Russian tanks would not come to liberate the workers and restore order—we have no territorial army to do the job. Can no one detect a pattern in the series of strikes which always seem to hit one vital part after another of our industrial output or export trade?

Are we to let the history of the 'thirties happen all over again, this time with psychological weapons, because we are too complacent to recognise an equally sinister threat to our freedom? Have we destroyed the bloody talons of the Nazi Eagle only to allow ourselves to be hugged to death between the equally bloody claws of the Red Bear?

Once again the writing is on the wall, the symbol is different, but it too adorns the crimson banner of dictatorship. Because Prime Ministers and Press proclaim a week to be a long time in politics, must cunning take the place of wisdom and focus the eyes and ears of our people on the trees in our backyards, calmly to wait the coming of 'Great Birnam wood to high Dunsinane hill'?

Index